Praise for All Day DevOps: The World's Largest DevOps Conference

D1571397

"Simple, rich content, open discussion in real time happening around the world. WOW!"

"You never fail to bring your community a boatload of AWESOME!"

"Everything is telling me I should go to bed, but my desire for knowledge is keeping me glued to my screen for #alldaydevops."

"I'd love to know how you pulled this off on such a massive scale."

"Tons of amazing sessions, flawless organization. Kudos to everyone involved."

"These were great sessions, and I will work my butt off to take this great advice back to my organization."

"ADDO is one of the best world wide learning conferences. You guys never disappoint!"

"FOMO with multitrack is so real! Good thing we have recordings."

"It has been an amazing and informative learning experience."

"Great talks going on since 'early' morning. It has been
great knowledge sharing experience. Thank you ADDO."

"This was great! Next year, I will have all of my
employees to sign up to the sessions they want."

"As a first timer, I thought this was great.
Congrats for bringing these ideas to the
masses in a highly accessible way."

"Thanks for making the world a better
place, one event at a time."

"Year after year I see an overwhelming amount
of support and excitement around this one
event. It's my favorite of the year."

"Ya'll are amazing. I'm already looking
forward to next year."

"You have once again outdone yourself. Congratulations."

"It was awesome!!"

Voices of All Day DevOps, Volume 2

FEEDBACK LOOPS

ISBN: 9798645690878
Imprint: All Day DevOps Press

Publisher:
All Day DevOps Press
48 Wall Street, 5th Floor
New York, NY 10005

www.alldaydevops.com

Voices of All Day DevOps, Volume 2

FEEDBACK LOOPS

Table of Contents

Introduction

by Derek Weeks

Introduction

I've now spent 43 days in isolation with my family. From the best I can judge, there are at least 28 more days of this routine ahead of us. Little did I know five years ago, the idea Mark Miller and I spawned walking around a conference in San Francisco would be attempted by countless organizations around the world as the realities of a COVID-19 pandemic set in. Virtual conferences would become a necessity of the times.

Mark and I came up with the idea to build an industry conference for "everyone else." We were walking the halls of yet another DevOps event we had attended that year. Our travels had taken us to over 25 conferences in the previous twelve months. We were catching up with friends, meeting new colleagues from across the community, comparing notes from sessions we had just attended, and sharing new perspectives on the journeys we were all undertaking. But as much as the community had gathered for this event — in reality, the experience was more exclusive than inclusive.

For example, I remember sitting down at that event for a conversation with Shannon Lietz from Intuit and two other members of her team. It was also the first conference where I had met with Julie Tsai — then at Walmart Labs and now at Roblox. In conversations with Shannon, Julie, and many others, I learned that while they were at the conference attending sessions, meeting others, and learning throughout the event, there were hundreds and sometimes thousands of their colleagues who remained back at the office. As much as post-conference notes, shared slide decks, and trip reports could give those folks some new ideas or spark conversations, their experiences would never capture the same value as being there.

That sparked the idea for Mark and me. If we took the conference presentations online, created conversation zones that would mimic conference "hallway tracks," and made the experience accessible to everyone, we could reach thousands — maybe tens of thousands — of people. That idea became All Day DevOps.

Each year, All Day DevOps hosts an annual conference attracting more than 40,000 participants from well over 100 countries. A team of 200 speakers, track moderators, and volunteers contribute to running the conference over 24 hours. It is not surprising to see 100,000 conversations logged by conference attendees in our free Slack workspace. We work hard to deliver on our promise of a "no vendor pitch" conference environment. Every session is delivered online is free — thanks to our generous sponsors.

Over the years, we've continuously improved the experience for our community. We've made every session from each of our conferences available free and on demand. We've produced hundreds of blog posts covering DevOps lessons learned. We've encouraged women, minorities, and others of diverse backgrounds to take part and share their knowledge. Working with our community members, we've introduced new tracks, topics, and workshops. We've encouraged participants to not watch alone, but to gather teams or local communities to participate and learn together. In 2019, All Day DevOps participants self-organized over 185 satellite viewing parties around the world — the largest of which gathered nearly 1,000 people.

From the beginning, All Day DevOps was designed to be inclusive. We built a platform, invited experts and everyday practitioners, and invited the world. The stories shared in this book are theirs; authentic, honest, and educational. The stories share the experiences of blazing new trails, failing at something again and again (and sometimes succeeding), and driving innovation. The stories document the lessons learned, reveal the roadmaps, and sometimes share the code or architectures used to make it happen. We share these stories here with you to help you learn, spark new ideas, or to introduce you to someone new. The people that shared their stories are all still available in our Slack workspace for you to chat with, ask questions of, and to collaborate with. The experience of this book does not stop within these pages and I would like to encourage you to reach out to any of the people featured across these chapters.

Back to the realities of our new COVID-19 influenced world. It was 43 days ago that Mark and I were working to assemble nearly 1,000 executives and managers at State Farm. We had assembled a small group of All Day DevOps speakers for a special on-site conference on their campus. With lockdowns and travel restrictions being initiated across companies and countries, we had no choice but to postpone that in person event until another time.

Within hours or days — it all blurs now — other conferences that I was speaking at in the Spring, like O'Reilly's Software Architecture Summit and DevopsDays SLC, were pulled off the map or postponed. For many of my friends across the industry who speak occasionally or regularly at conferences, their travel was grinding to a halt too. Their roles as evangelists, advocates, thought leaders, and educators were impacted abruptly. They were all grounded.

I knew at that point, we could pull something off to help those friends and continue to serve the DevOps community around the world. For the past five years, we've assembled people that could not reach one another in person. We had done it with help from the community. We knew how to organize it. We knew how to produce it. And we knew how to reach thousands of people with whom to share experiences. Within thirty days, we delivered a special All Day DevOps "Spring Break Edition" to 7,000 people. Stories from those practitioners are also shared within these pages.

Serving the DevOps community from afar is why we started All Day DevOps. It was not a COVID-19 response plan, it was a community inclusion and education plan. Our original idea continues to serve the DevOps community with education for all. The stories within this book are representative of that idea, our values, and experiences.

If you are one of those who have joined us over the years, thank you. If you are new to our community, welcome. The chapters here can be read in any particular order. Find a topic that interests you, dive in, learn something, and apply the knowledge you gain. Enjoy your own journey through *Feedback Loops, The Voices of All Day DevOps, Volume 2.*

Derek E. Weeks | Co-founder, All Day DevOps

CHAPTER 1

Crossing the River by Feeling the Stones

presented by Simon Wardley

CHAPTER 1

Crossing the River by Feeling the Stones

The path of knowing very little to eventually gaining understanding is a tough one, but luckily, we have a map for it. Here's what one CEO's path to understanding looked like:

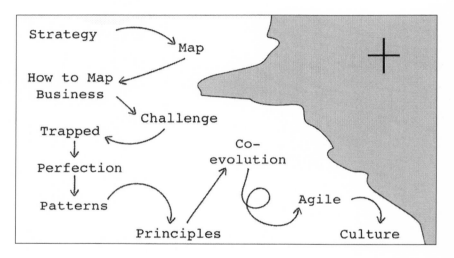

But of course, we need more detail! So first, let's look at strategy.

Reading all the books on strategy doesn't necessarily lead to understanding strategy. But the strategy cycle from Sun Tzu's five factors, taken from his book *The Art of War*, identifies the following components.

- ▶ Purpose
- ▶ Landscape
- ▶ Climate
- ▶ Doctrine
- ▶ Leadership

But ultimately, we still need to understand the why. Without understanding why we move through these stages, we can't create a valid strategy.

After understanding the cycle of strategy, we need to look at the map that gets us there. But what makes a map? With maps, space has meaning. And it can change the context of a graph by giving it a compass, or a direction that provides additional focus.

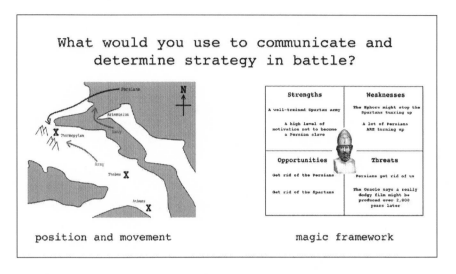

Here are some of the maps we have in business:

▶ Mind maps

▶ Business process maps

▶ System maps

And what do all these maps have in common? They're imperfect. They're representations of the real world but cannot provide strategy. They're all just graphs. They lack direction or a compass. So what can we do instead?

Mapping a Business: Tea

Take, for example, selling a cup of tea. The cup of tea has needs — the tea leaves, a cup, and hot water. The kettle also has needs, like power and a tap. Once we have these anchors mapped out, we begin to develop a chain of needs.

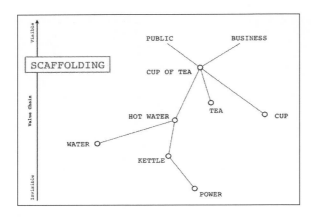

So now that we have an example of what anchors and needs might look like, where do we go next? We're missing additional information. Our maps should show movement, which we can describe as change itself.

But how do we do that? Theoretically, it should be easy. Looking at the concepts described in the book *Diffusion of Innovations* by Everett Rogers makes it seem simple. Taking in innovation, product, and other components should result in showing the movement. But it's not actually that simple. Things diffuse, but they also evolve.

To illustrate this, let's take a look at smartphone adoption over time. It would have been difficult to know when in the cycle the phone would become ubiquitous in the market.

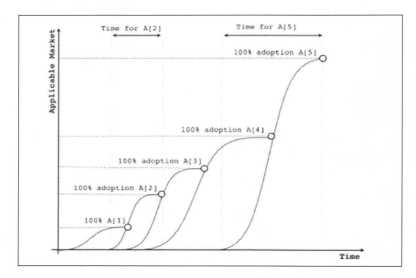

The point of stability marks where the product becomes ubiquitous in the market. This helps us understand movement.

Once we've defined movement, we can add that to the axis at the bottom.

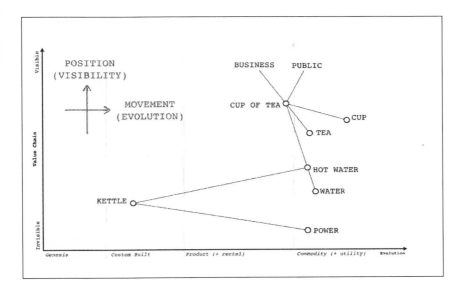

On a single map, we have a multitude of factors that affect your product. Here's how that might look for our tea example.

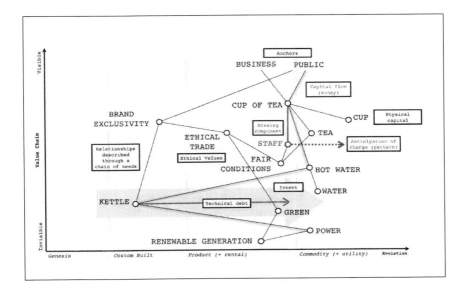

Mapping a Business: Insurance

Now, imagine that an insurance company had a problem. They had a bottleneck in providing their service to the customer. The solution they invested in and drove towards involved advanced robotics. That seems like a heavy-weight solution for an insurance company. Why was that the solution they drove towards?

The answer came out when they mapped their business. With the map, an interesting discovery surfaced. The need for robotics stemmed from not a need that the customer had. Instead, it came from the company's decision to use custom-built racks. And because of these custom-built racks, their thought process led them down the path of working within that constraint. And robotics was the only visible solution. However, a solution of going to standard racks could improve their process flow and eliminate the need for continued customization.

Going to a standard offering instead of a custom-built one allowed them to find the right optimization. They were trying to optimize a flow that required highly technical solutions due to assumptions made long ago. And this was made clear by mapping it out on the bottleneck.

"Past Success Breeds Inertia"

Once we understand the landscape, we need to look for patterns. In other words, we need to identify the rules for the game.

Past success breeds inertia. Take Blockbuster vs. Netflix. Who had a website first? Blockbuster. First with video on the web? Blockbuster. First with streaming? Blockbuster. First to bankrupt? Blockbuster.

It wasn't a lack of innovation that brought Blockbuster down. It was a business model focused on late fees. Netflix came in and changed the business model. They succeeded where Blockbuster couldn't.

Let's look at a different example. By taking a systems diagram and creating a map, the company Fotango developed the first serverless environment. Unfortunately, executives disagreed with the strategy and pushed the company in the direction of 3D TV. We can all now see that was a bad bet. Past success was their downfall.

Efficiency Leads to Innovation

Certain people will say that you need agile everywhere. Others say that it has its place. Where does agile map?

Going back to our example with the insurance company, building custom racks resulted in inefficient processes and bottlenecks.

Instead of customizing everything and building it ourselves, we should focus on what matters. So outsource utility to suppliers, use off-the-shelf products, and then build the components that have meaning in-house using agile methodologies.

Closing

As a final thought, let's look at the current push to automate all the things. We use DevOps, agile, cloud technologies, Kubernetes, and everything else to improve the efficiency of our process. However, adding automation and DevOps to your processes can speed up segments of your process. *But without mapping the entire problem, we're solving the wrong problem.*

Don't focus on optimizing the process flow. Instead, focus on evolving the process flow. ∎

ABOUT THE PRESENTER

Simon Wardley is a former CEO, former advisory board member of startups (all now acquired by US Giants), a fellow of Open Europe, inventor of Wardley Mapping, a regular conference speaker and a researcher for the Leading Edge Forum. He uses mapping in his research for the LEF covering areas from Serverless to Nation State competition whilst also advising/teaching LEF clients on mapping, strategy, organisation and leadership.

Summary provided by Sylvia Fronczak.

Go to bit.ly/2020addo-wardley *to watch the entire presentation.*

CHAPTER 2

#adidoescode
Where DevOps Meets the
Sporting Goods Industry

presented by Fernando Cornago

CHAPTER 2

#adidoescode
Where DevOps Meets the Sporting Goods Industry

Adidas is a huge company, bringing home about 2.3 billion annually in operating profit, with the help of its almost 60,000 employees around the world, of which 51% are men and 49% are women. Adidas believes that, through sport, we have the power to change lives, by improving health and improving people's life prospects.

Currently, software is changing sports. Not only how we practice sports but also how we consume sports. Is Adidas a software company? Definitely not, since all of its revenue comes from selling physical products. But it needs to start behaving like a software company. Why? There are studies that show that, in the next 10 years, 50% of companies are going to be displaced by new companies. And if you take a look at the trends, you'll see that most of these new companies are either technology companies or traditional companies that have mastered software development and delivery.

Even though Adidas isn't a software company in the traditional sense, it already employs advanced techniques in software delivery since it builds different applications more than ten thousand times a day.

The Role of IT
What is the role of IT in all of this? In short, to provide speed and quality. In other words, technology should allow our teams to get closer to the business and provide value for the company, delivering value faster, at what we call "sustainable speed."

All of this is particularly important for Adidas because of the industry in which it operates — retail — which is particularly competitive. In fact, if you look at the results from the "State of DevOps" report, you can see that the only industry where there is a correlation between software performance and business results is retail. In retail, you'd better be good at software or you're dead.

Cloud-Native Platforms for DevOps

There are certain capabilities the cloud platform needs to have in order to enable an efficient DevOps strategy:

▶ **On-demand and self-service:** Eams need to be able to run these platforms whenever they want.

▶ **Scalable and elastic:** The platform needs to scale up and down depending on the variable usage.

▶ **Pay per use:** The users are paying for what they use, so everyone works with performance and efficiency in mind. That allows the creation of a product budget: the team owns the cost and the revenue they generate.

▶ **Transparent and measurable:** Observability is essential, so the platform needs to be open in both directions. That means that users of the platform need to be able to see metrics of how the platform is behaving. For software development teams it's also useful to see the metrics of users using the platform.

▶ **Open/inner source:** Not only because we need to use open-source software, but a platform is also only as good as it's open for the team.

Adidas Digital Priorities

As explained before, Adidas isn't a software company, which means it has to carefully decide how to allocate its resources when it comes to technological initiatives.

One of the most important of such initiatives is what Adidas calls "Digital Tech Foundation," which is the base for all of the other digital initiatives, from digital commerce, to consumer engagement and membership, and E2E digital creation.

There Are Challenges: Bringing the Business Onboard

Adidas DevOps teams were facing the challenge of bringing the business on board, and really convincing others of the importance of all of those new initiatives. Then, one day, they finally realized that the capabilities their platforms have are the same properties that are ingrained in Adidas' DNA from the very beginning, 70 years ago.

Here is a summary of the DevOps capabilities that exist in the Adidas company:

▶ ODP

▶ FDP

▶ BDP

▶ API

▶ Testing

▶ Monitoring

▶ CI/CD

▶ Robotic Process Automation

What DevOps professionals at Adidas found out is that many if not most of these capabilities already align with the original "DNA" of the company. For instance, testing. Testing has always been a core value of Adidas since its founder would himself go to athletes to test their shoes.

DevOps Cup

In 2019, Adidas organized the DevOps Cup: a competition with 25 teams, 220 participants, 12 mentors, 4 jury members, and 9 months of duration, with the goal to find out which teams could have the best transformation.

The Cup brought remarkable results for Adidas. Here is a brief summary of what was accomplished:

▶ Build time for the Adidas app decreased by 3,720 minutes, total

▶ Fewer bugs in production due to more test automation

▶ Double-digit million euros in sales increase

▶ A decrease in the cost per case in consumer service

▶ Consumer service decrease of 40% of their manual testing, and 60% of the total human effort involved in testing

▶ Creation of the DevOps Maturity Framework to assess the teams and to help mentors

Cultural Changes

But for sure the most dramatic change has been in culture. Before, DevOps was the responsibility of a few teams. Now, every feature team does DevOps. The use of open-source technologies has skyrocketed in the company, as well as collaborations between different teams. ■

ABOUT THE PRESENTER

Fernando Cornago is a passionate team builder, agile and lean practitioner, amateur software architect and a rusty coder. Holding Masters Degree in Computer Science and Teaching, extended with Executive Development in M.I.T. and Harvard Business School. He's a connector and community builder. Obsessed with measurement, feedback cycles and Continuous Improvement, he has devoted his entire life leading software teams, in Companies such as GFT or HP. He joined Adidas in 2015, first leading Global Software Development and later Platform Engineering. Playing a key role in designing and heading up the creation and setup of the successful Software Engineering IT Hub adidas has created in Zaragoza, Spain.

Summary provided by Carlos Schults.

Go to bit.ly/2020addo-cornago *to watch the entire presentation.*

CHAPTER 3

The Intersection of Communication and Technology

presented by Emily Freeman

CHAPTER 3

The Intersection of Communication and Technology

What is our progress in DevOps? When the DevOps movement started, the world was doing weekly releases at best. But the speed of change in technology is much faster. Still, the real holdup is us — people.

DevOps can be defined this way: An engineering culture of collaboration, ownership, and learning with the purpose of accelerating the software development life cycle from ideation to production.

When DevOps is done properly, it brings people together. Despite the popularity of tools and processes, it's really about people and communication. It's very similar to — more of an extension of — the agile manifesto and its twelve principles.

Devops is an engineering culture of collaboration, ownership, and learning with the purpose of accelerating the software development life cycle from ideation to production.

Even if you aren't nailing the twelve principles, as most of us aren't, that's OK. It's the recognition that's important. We can still strive to achieve this really difficult goal. And in 2008, Andrew Clay Shafer talked to Patrick Dubois about the frustrations of the hand-off to operations that were still part of agile. They launched DevOps Days, which was the true birth of DevOps.

DevOps Is Making the Industry Better

Today, DevOps is here to stay in a big way. It permeates every fiber of our technology. The State of DevOps Report in 2014 proves it.

✓	✓	✓	✓	✓
Peer-reviewed change approval process	Version control for all production artifacts	Proactive monitoring	High-trust organizational culture	Win-win relationship between dev and ops

Findings from the 2014 State of DevOps Report

Furthermore, organizations were delivering more often with lower rates of failure.

Then, in 2017, the same report recognized that things got even better. And now, in 2019, the top performers slowed things down a bit. This could be due to the way the data was measured or it could be due to reactions to change. For example, additional processes may have been added to allow for more control over the production.

SURVEY QUESTIONS	ELITE PERFORMERS	HIGH PERFORMERS	MEDIUM PERFORMERS	LOW PERFORMERS
Deployment Frequency	On-demand (multiple deploys per day)	Between once per day and once per week	Between once per week and once per month	Between once per month and once every six months
Lead Time for Changes	Less than one day	Between one day and one week	Between one week and one month	Between one month and six months
Time to Restore Service	Less than one hour	Less than one day	Less than one day	Between one week and one month
Change Failure Rate	0-15%	0-15%	0-15%	46-60%

2019 State of DevOps Survey Results

Most of Us Are Still Figuring it Out

Although DevOps is taking hold in more and more organizations, it's not necessarily being done well. DevOps is hard. It's especially hard to shift mindsets to a whole new paradigm. It takes time, patience, and practice.

How Can We Get There?

One way is to use CI/CD. But this is tough to spin up since it requires a robust test suite. But you benefit by having an accelerated feedback loop. It's also important to have great interpersonal communications because of the way things move. Members of teams have to trust each other!

The CI/CD tools you use depends on your tech stacks and environments. Engineers need to be trained on the tools.

FEATURE FLAGS

Feature flags are a way to turn features on and off in production. The code can be deployed and running in production, but it isn't released until it's switched on. This means the technical team can actually get ahead of other departments like marketing. When the organization is ready to release, it's just a flip of a switch.

DOCUMENTATION

If code and tests are getting ahead of documentation, things can start to drift.

TALK TO PEOPLE

Coordination is just as important as CI/CD tools. This takes communication and collaboration.

What Is the Cloud?

The cloud isn't some magical unicorn in the sky... it's just a way to say "someone else's servers." Sure, when we run DevOps in the cloud, we remove some barriers such as cost and space. But we should be cautious not to lose focus on what's important: people, process, then technology, in that order. The cloud falls into the last category.

Trust, Space, and Time

In order to really become a high performing team, you need people that trust each other. Process can help nudge trust in the right direction, but it still takes space and time to build real trust. Without trust, the speed of change can push people into burnout.

The Value of Diversity

Diversity is vital to producing an environment that enables innovation, success, and happiness. Diversity comes in many forms. The surface diversity of gender, race, and age is just one type of diversity. Though it's important, we should not lose focus on other types of diversity that have to do with life experiences, perspectives, and knowledge.

The Future

To those on the bleeding edge, or even the cutting edge, it may seem like DevOps is dead. But the story is much different for so many who work in enterprises and more long-lived companies who have accumulated a host of technical debt. For those companies that have a host of processes ingrained in their culture, change is much harder than it is for a newer company, a startup, or a company that lives by producing software.

DevOps is alive and needs to continue to grow with a people-focused perspective. ∎

ABOUT THE PRESENTER

Emily Freeman is a technologist and a storyteller who helps engineering teams improve their velocity. As the author of DevOps for Dummies, she believes the biggest challenges facing developers aren't technical, but human. Her mission in life is to transform technology organizations by creating company cultures in which diverse, collaborative teams can thrive. Emily leads the modern operations advocacy team at Microsoft and lives in Denver with her daughter. You can find Emily on Twitter at @editingemily.

Summary provided by Phil Vuollet.

Go to bit.ly/2020addo-freeman *to watch the entire presentation.*

CHAPTER 4

Damming a
97-Year-Old Waterfall
Transforming to DevOps
at State Farm

presented by Kevin O'Dell and Jeremy Castle

CHAPTER 4

Damming a 97-Year-Old Waterfall
Transforming to DevOps at State Farm

Jeremy Castle and Kevin O'Dell, DevOps leaders at State Farm Insurance, help teams understand a new way of working that creates high performing teams through a DevOps mindset. In this chapter, they'll take us on a journey through their DevOps transformation at State Farm.

State Farm is the 36th-ranked Fortune 500 company and has been around since 1922. They have 83.4 million policies and accounts. Their enterprise technology department alone is composed of 6,000 employees and over 2,000 web applications. There are more than 1,200 product teams to support their systems.

Workspace to Production in 24 Hours

On Jeremy's first day on the job, his boss challenged him to get code from a developer workstation to production in less than 24 hours. After many years of never seeing projects make it to production, this seems like an overwhelming initiative at first. But it was a simple, tangible challenge that gave him and his teammates a North Star to drive towards.

To see how to change, he had to figure out how State Farm works. So he created a value stream map of the entire process State Farm takes to bring code from inception to production. In this, there were close to 155 processes with almost an equal number of handoffs to other teams.

It would take over 1,500 hours to get code all the way through this value stream. But at least now they could physically get their heads around how software gets delivered. Some bottlenecks were obvious to see. Others lurked deeper. This value stream map laid the foundation for future change.

There are two mountains they had to climb over to get their 24-hour-to-production goal. First, there was the lack of automation in many of their processes. But they also had to deal with their change processes, at both the department and project levels. Often the only reason these processes existed was because "this is the way we've always done it."

So they reset the process from the ground up. They automated much of the change processes, lowering production time from days to hours.

MANUAL	VS	AUTOMATED
13	Change Management Process	2
59	Manual Fields	4
6	Roles Involved in Change Creation and Approval	2
3	Leader Approvals Required	1
14+	Manual Implementaiton Tasks (manual fields)	0
Multiple Weeks	Change Process	Hours

The change process at State Farm.

How State Farm Improved

But how exactly did State Farm enable this improvement to happen? Well, when you have all this automation and security, you can't forget about the people. State Farm had to get their people to adopt the DevOps way of working.

One way they created a DevOps culture was to adopt the "dojo model" that Target had. It's not a classroom but rather an open place for learning based on the knowledge people currently had. This type of change is the type that will get executives excited, and that's what happened at State Farm — the developers there found support from executives.

With the automation and the people's buy-in in place, they next needed to look hard at their team structures. They decided to go from projects to products. Products never end and need to have full support and ownership, and they designed that into their teams.

Challenges

Climbing the DevOps mountain was not without its avalanches and steep hills. They still had dates and people who were used to waterfall projects.

Here are the top five things that they encountered.

1. **When everybody owns something, nobody owns it.** They were playing feature "plinko," which meant people were working on things they didn't understand well. So more ownership was pushed to each

team in building their own pipelines, logging, and tooling. The biggest challenge were the product owners, who had to learn more deeply the products their team worked on.

2. **It might be embarrassing. Your first releases will be pretty tough.** You have to take the time upfront to build in the automation and resiliency needed to produce the new functionality, and that may mean lower initial features released.

3. **It's tempting to have a separate DevOps team.** State Farm had to push hard to help enable teams to adopt DevOps ideas without siloing into a team solely focused on Ops or on building the automation pipelines. Leaders had to enable and coach, but the product teams execute on the ideas.

4. **You have to flatten the layers.** Teams need to be cross-functional so that communication is clear and effective. For example, architects need to be embedded in product teams, not as a separate layer above them.

5. **Learn to unlearn.** There's so much old waterfall thinking that people had to overcome. And people had to be intentional about changing to a different way of thinking. For example, instead of obsessing over code duplication, they needed to focus on decoupling that code.

Conclusion

Despite the challenges State Farm faced, they had the right leadership support and passion to continue to push forth to a better way of deploying software. Customers, business stakeholders, and software professionals are all happier as a result. ■

ABOUT THE PRESENTERS

Kevin O'Dell has served in many IT roles at State Farm and is currently a Technology Director within the Home and Auto Insurance area. As a former developer who has spent many nights and weekends fixing production issues [which he often caused], Kevin has a great appreciation for all aspects of building and running critical business applications. In his current role, he leads a suite of product teams responsible for developing and operating data centric applications and is also tasked with the enablement and adoption of DevOps practices across many product areas. Kevin is all about creating a culture of awesomeness by challenging teams to innovate and try things, pushing new-aged mindsets, and refusing to use his Director office so he can sit with product teams.

Jeremy Castle is an Engineering Director at State Farm. He started his career as a software developer and most recently took on the role of Engineering Director over State Farm's App Dev Practices. He has seen many sides of the development world, being a developer himself. He has helped teams adopt continuous delivery and agile methodologies and is now leading the teams that are responsible for enabling the developer tooling and practices to make DevOps successful at State Farm. He is also an advocate for building a fun and transparent culture by using his ninja skills to sneak a ping pong table past security.

Summary provided by Mark Henke.

Go to bit.ly/2020addo-odell *to watch the entire presentation.*

CHAPTER 5

Why Happy Developers Create More Secure Code

presented by DJ Schleen and Derek Weeks

CHAPTER 4

Why Happy Developers Create More Secure Code

The industry has collected a lot of data over the years, from what makes an organization high performing, to what makes developers happy. Today, we'll look at some data in the spirit of W. Edwards Deming, a quality specialist who loved to dive deep into data.

We will look at survey results from people across the community over a period of months. This data comes from multiple organizations that helped build the 2020 DevSecOps Survey.

A Quick History of Surveys

Sonatype and its partners have been surveying people for a few years now. They started in 2014, near the time the Heartbleed vulnerability was discovered. Since then, the survey focused more on software security.

Who Responded to This Survey?

In the most recent iteration of the survey, 5,045 people shared their responses across 102 countries and across many different industries, although mostly in technology. Respondents identified what their role was in their organization. There have been some changes in the survey year over year.

This year saw a rise in people who call themselves "DevSecOps specialists." It also had more people slotting themselves into security-focused roles. This says that more people are thinking about security as being at the forefront of their job.

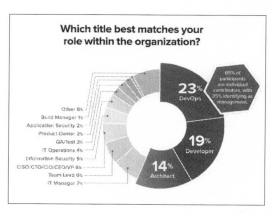

Which title best matches your role within the organization?

23% DevOps

19% Developer

14% Architect

65% of participants are individual contributors, with 35% identifying as management.

Other 8%
Build Manager 1%
Application Security 2%
Product Owner 2%
QA/Test 3%
IT Operations 4%
Information Security 5%
CISO/CTO/CIO/CEO/VP 8%
Team Lead 6%
IT Manager 7%

Differing Perspective

In this survey, Sonatype wanted to hone in on who was just starting their DevSecOps journey and who was considered elite in the industry. There's a chance we can find some interesting data by delving into these differences.

Sonatype also strived to contrast those who were happy in their organizations versus who may be dissatisfied in their current positions. They then looked at the characteristics of those results.

To supplement this contrast, there was a Gallup poll that surveyed employee engagement in the US from 2000 to 2018:

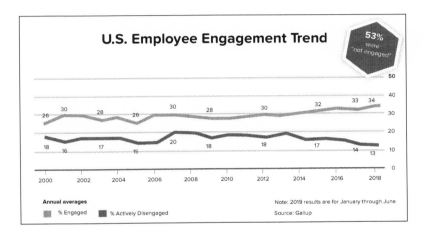

It shows that over 50% of people are actively disengaged from their organization and the work that they do.

There is common wisdom that says happier employees will make the organization as a whole more effective, and this shows that many companies have improvements to make.

Thinking About Culture

In general, there are three categories of culture in an organization:

- ▶ Pathological, or power-oriented.
- ▶ Bureaucratic, or rule-oriented.
- ▶ Generative, or performance-oriented.

Organizations should strive to be generative. Generative organizations are highly cooperative and are constantly improving their effectiveness through learning and risk sharing.

Non-generative organizations will create employee dissatisfaction. For example, blaming a team for not meeting sprint commitments will dishearten developers. They may actually pull less work from the backlog in order to ensure they do not get blamed again.

Team Friction

Sonatype's survey asked participants who cause the most friction versus satisfaction for them:

The survey, combined with the Gallup poll, found that happy developers said there was no friction. But 80% of the employees said management was the biggest source of friction and were dissatisfied and disengaged from their work.

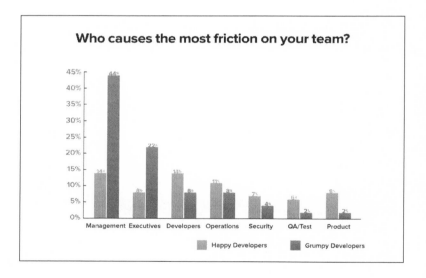

Reducing Unhealthy Friction

When we talk about friction, take into account that not all friction is bad. Friction can be healthy, slowing things down in order to increase quality. When friction is found, it is often good to automate processes so that preferred protocols are followed more often.

When it comes to unhealthy friction, we want to look at cultural aspects that can affect friction for better or for worse. For example, a caring culture can perform highly at communication and engagement but have friction in over-consensus and decision by committee. In contrast, a results-oriented culture can produce high stress but can achieve high throughput of software delivery.

Job Satisfaction and DevOps

We know that DevOps practices reduce unhealthy friction and automate healthy friction, but how does that affect job satisfaction?

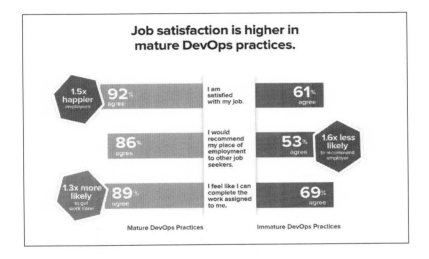

Survey results showed that organizations with mature DevOps practices had much higher job satisfaction. In fact, more than 82% of developers with mature DevOps practices said they would recommend their company to potential job seekers.

Happy Developers and Security

How are these happy developers thinking about security? Survey results show that they are informed 1.3x more by tooling and informed 3.8x less by rumor when compared to unhappy developers.

Also, satisfied developers actively research and pursue security knowledge for their teams:

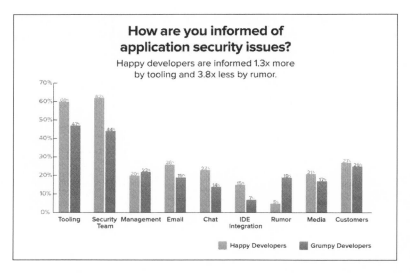

Happy developers educate themselves more frequently. This leads to learning and changing their organization for the better. Happy developers have more e-learning available to them and are more likely to have security training in some fashion. Finally, happy developers act as a first line of defense in security.

How Can We Encourage Happier Developers to Learn More Security?

How can we help developers go from grumpy to happy with regard to security? We can take one person from each team and create a security champion program. Invite everyone, but have these members be the champions for learning security. Host it once a month and supplement it with security training sessions.

According to the Sonatype survey, developers who receive training like this will be happier and more engaged.

Deployment and Vulnerability Exposure

With both unhappy and happy developers, at least 55% said they deploy to production at least once a week. This is a significant improvement over past surveys.

In fact, over the past decade, the average time from a vulnerability being discovered to when it is patched has dropped from 45 to 3 days.

We are seeing these happier developers actively reducing vulnerability exposure rates through mature DevOps practices like fast, automated deployments.

In the open source community, we are seeing breaches continue to drop, but they still occur frequently.

One in five open source components still have breaches.

To help combat this, we can see that organizations with mature DevOps practices are more aware of breaches than ones with immature practices by 4%–9%.

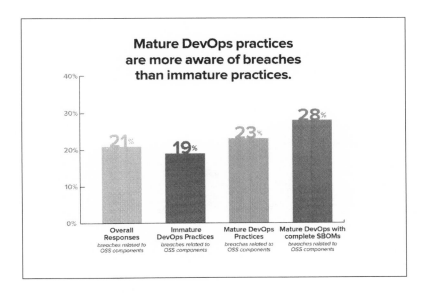

What Security Tools Make People More Productive?

The survey finds that automation is key to enabling both security and productivity. Many of the tools that have a big impact are ones like application firewalls — tools that automatically detect and block vulnerable communication. Productive teams have these tools properly integrated. It is hard work, but mature teams make the investment.

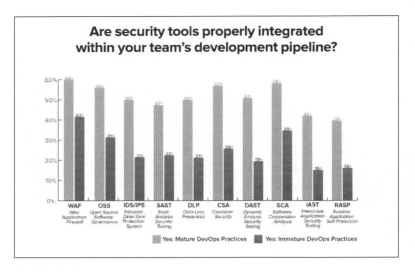

Conclusion

The most recent survey results revealed a lot of information about how happier developers are more productive and produce more secure software. Happiness influences includes everything from the business culture, to the kinds of automation in place, and what tools are integrated into the development process. Happier developers are also well-trained and actively engaged in their team's security practices. ■

ABOUT THE PRESENTERS

Derek E. Weeks is a huge advocate of applying proven supply chain management principles into DevOps practices to improve efficiencies and sustain long-lasting competitive advantages. He currently serves as vice president and DevOps advocate at Sonatype, creators of the Nexus Repository Manager and the global leader in solutions for software supply chain automation.

Derek is also the co-founder of All Day DevOps, an online community of 40,000 IT professionals, and the lead researcher behind the annual State of the Software Supply Chain report for the DevOps industry.

In 2018, Derek was recognized by DevOps.com as the "Best DevOps Evangelist" for his work in the community.

DJ Schleen is a DevSecOps pioneer, creator of The DevSecOps Experiments, a DevSecOps Evangelist, and a Security Architect. He provides thought leadership to organizations adopting DevSecOps practices worldwide. DJ specializes in designing DevSecOps pipelines and automating security controls in DevOps environments. He is also an ethical hacker and performs significant R&D work in Moving Target Defense.

DJ has worked to streamline the development practices for many Fortune 100 organizations by focusing on culture, technique, the right technology, and the goals of the business. He is an international speaker, blogger, instructor and author in the DevSecOps community where he encourages organizations to deeply integrate a culture of security and trust into their core values and product development journey.

Summary provided by Mark Henke.

Go to bit.ly/2020addo-weeks *to watch the entire presentation.*

CHAPTER 6

The Future of Software Security

Conversations You'll Need to Have

presented by Kate Healy

CHAPTER 6

The Future of Software Security
Conversations You'll Need to Have

Why do the bad guys keep winning? There are misconceptions about who the bad guys even are. The public thinks of malicious hackers as guys dressed in a hoodie. But that's inaccurate — they look like you, or me.

Perhaps at one time, this vandalizing loner represented the biggest security threat. Back when hackers were people who, well, hacked, for the fun and thrill of it. But this isn't how things are today.

Why do we still have breaches, then?

1. Because of the way we think of security. It's not a gated state, but a process. "Am I secure?" is the wrong question.

2. Modern environments are extremely complex, and complexity is the enemy of security. Applications that we use have tens of millions of lines of code, with just as many opportunities for mistakes and misconfigurations.

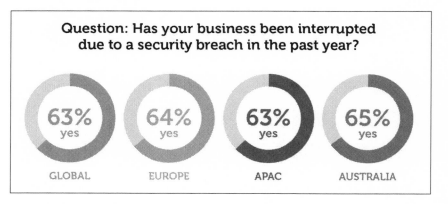

And we have a lot of breaches. As you can see above, no matter how/ where you slice it, nearly two thirds of companies have been interrupted by breaches. The three most common forms of attack are web application attacks, business email compromises, and human error.

Years ago, when Kate would say that she worked in cybersecurity, people didn't really understand this very well. And, she and her team were "kept in the basement." They were usually brought in reluctantly and too late for prevention, and organizations viewed them as drag on software development.

These days, security has more of a first class role, and the rise of agile methodologies and DevOps have helped. But there are still challenges and a long way to go.

Consider that security is really a form of risk, which is a very business-facing concern. Mention risk in the C-suite, and you'll have everyone's attention. So it's interesting that security — risk management at its core — is delegated to inside of the IT organization. And this becomes even more fascinating and disturbing when you consider that two of the three most common attack vectors involve human error and social engineering.

Here's an interesting example.

A newly installed CFO receives an email apparently from the CEO, requesting a funds transfer, and complies. She sends a text to the CEO to confirm, and the CEO immediately calls and raises an alert, which surfaces that this was, in fact, a false email. When you think about this, an organization can solve for this just as easily, if not more so, with process than with technology.

Cybersecurity is an Enterprise-wide risk management issue, not just an IT issue.

National Association of Corporate Directors

And this demands a two-pronged approach to security, involving technology and people.

Because security is, in fact, an organization-wide concern, we're seeing a rise in the Chief Information Security Officer (CISO) role. This role does not report to the CIO, but rather directly to the CEO: a development which allows the security organization to be far more cross-cutting.

As a result, cybersecurity organizations are taking on more of a governance and advisory role, meaning that DevOps teams might find themselves more hands-on with security, engaging security folks in a more advisory capacity.

But that shift has led to confusion about what all the cybersecurity group actually owns. Things wind up falling to them by default.

We often confuse security with privacy, even though they are not the same thing.

With security, we tend to talk about protecting the data and the system along three axes: confidentiality, integrity, and availability. With privacy, we're more interested in protecting data about an individual. How do we collect information, disclose, and access it? And what kind of quality of data do we have?

However, there are some commonalities regarding controls. This includes activities like installing firewalls, putting authentication in place, etc. This results in similar processes and institutions and the data and privacy concern falling on the cybersecurity team by default.

This is a common, but not the only, example of things falling to the cybersecurity organization. They might inherit responsibility for regulatory compliance and other concerns as well, when people don't know where else to go.

Risk Is Not Bad

All of these concerns that may fall to the cybersecurity team revolve around the idea of risk: security, privacy, regulatory compliance, etc. And, while businesses clearly want to minimize and control risk, risk itself is not inherently bad.

In order to accomplish things and get ahead, businesses have to take risks. So risk management becomes not about eliminating risk, but minimizing the impact of what happens when things go wrong. And this is best done by aligning policies and activities with minimizing that impact. ■

ABOUT THE PRESENTER

Kate Healy is the Principal Cybersecurity Strategist at Telstra Enterprise where she works with the CISOs of Australia's largest organisations, understanding their cyber strategy and advising on industry trends and innovations. With almost two decades global experience, including 5 years in Singapore, her skills in cybersecurity, infrastructure and risk management have helped organisations better understand and reduce their cyber risk.

Summary provided by Erik Dietrich.

Go to bit.ly/2020addo-healy *to watch the entire presentation.*

CHAPTER 7

Hints and Glimmers of Things to Come

presented by Patrick Debois

CHAPTER 7

Hints and Glimmers of Things to Come

As interesting as the DevOps pipeline is, we're going to look at what lies beyond it. Many teams see the product backlog as a point of entry. But if your delivery pipeline works well enough, what's the next bottleneck? To answer that, we can look at other departments in our organization.

Hint 1: Fixing Sales Pipeline Bottlenecks

The first department we can find bottlenecks is sales. How can we have an agile sales pipeline that feeds into our backlog? A book by Justin Roff-Marsh called *The Machine* presents some ideas.

There's often a sales process with a lot of players in place. If you look closely, this process looks like a Kanban board, a key tool in DevOps! We want to connect this process to our backlog, which for most teams currently is akin to magic. How do we improve in quickly and reliably connecting them?

It feels like sales people are good mind readers when it comes to what customers want. But they often focus on the cost to make something instead of the value that thing will bring. Value and cost are often not connected.

Our backlog and our plan really starts at the beginning of the sales process. Like product roadmapping, sales has its own cone of uncertainty. As sales comes closer to an agreement, things become more certain. It's understood that estimates at this point are not promises.

The sales relationship is also continuous — it's not a project that gets "done." Yet contracts are written as if they have a stopping point. Agile delivery handles this well, but current sales processes don't.

We can help sales with their process by making things simpler. By making things simple, the value will be clearer and easier to sell.

Documentation also helps sell engagement. It's often ignored by developers, but making it a first-class concern will let us land more deals. This also makes customer support easier, which turns out to be a big reason why customers stay loyal to an organization.

Overall, DevOps and sales can go really well together.

Hint 2: DevOps Will Help Marketing

Beyond sales, there's another pipeline secretly connected to DevOps: the marketing pipeline. Without both marketing and sales, it would be really hard for software professionals to do their job. A key part to DevOps is automation, and marketing actually has some intriguing automation in its pipeline. They also track metrics, using things like website heat maps. They even apply lean principles to their pipeline.

An IT department can really help marketing. A great example of this can be found in the book *The Business Value of Developer Relations* by Mary Thengvall. It talks about this in depth.

Marketing is like IT's grandmother: they are developers' biggest fan! So keep a marketing perspective in mind when working in your DevOps pipeline.

Hint 3: Finance and DevOps Will Come Together

DevOps may benefit greatly from your budgeting approach. Instead of traditional budgets, look at using rolling budgets that are focused on product and value streams, instead of vertical functions like database, QA, etc.

DevOps and finance can go together beautifully with the right budgeting strategy.

Hint 4: Procurement Will be Agile

DevOps can benefit by being agile in your procurement. A great way to approach agile procurement is by using lean procurement canvases, which focus on the risks of finding the right partners and team fits.

How we approach serverless is a good example of agile procurement. In a serverless mindset, we procure a myriad of partner services, such as Gmail, to manage our system. This is superior to building most things ourselves.

As DevOps teams, we need to embrace our suppliers and the tools we procure from the outside.

Hint 5: We'll Have Agile HR

There's a manifesto for agile HR development to better support your employees. It hits upon collaborative networks, transparency, adaptability, and inspiration for managing people-centric challenges.

Automation is even invading HR. A great example is Shopify occasionally and automatically removing all recurring meetings off employee calendars to encourage more dynamic collaboration instead of traditional meetings.

Microsoft embraced agile HR by trying a four-day work week. Productivity shot up as a result of this experiment.

Hint 6: Team Room Practices Will Improve DevOps

There are some team room practices that are not strictly a part of DevOps but can increase performance. Mob programming is a great example. Everyone is collaborating and watching a problem at the same time, which can reduce handoffs and review times.

Wrapping Up

Overall, there are so many other departments that can have value for how DevOps works. And we can also give them value. Don't just stick to your own IT silo. Look at how you and your other departments, such as marketing, sales, and finance, can partner together. ∎

ABOUT THE PRESENTER

Patrick Debois coined the word 'DevOps' in 2009 by organizing the first DevOpsDays event. He organizes and speaks at conferences all over the world to collect and spread new ideas. As a pioneer he is always on the lookout for new ideas to implement and explore. He brings an exciting mix of technological background and hands-on business reality to the table. With Zender, a company he co-founded, Patrick currently builds a platform that allows brands and broadcasters to enter in a dialogue with large viewer audiences during live events. You can find Patrick on Twitter at @patrickdebois.

Summary provided by Mark Henke.

Go to bit.ly/2020addo-debois to watch the entire presentation.

CHAPTER 8

ZeroTrustOps
Securing at Scale

presented by Wendy Nather

CHAPTER 8

ZeroTrustOps
Securing at Scale

What is Zero Trust? With zero trust, you should assume everything on the network isn't safe. Yes, your internal network too. It doesn't mean that you shouldn't trust anyone ever. But you have to check trust explicitly. So even if it's on your network and got past your firewall, you still need to make sure it's safe.

The important thing to think about is that successful attackers look exactly like insiders. For example, an attacker once acquired a sys admin's credentials, came in through a VPN, and looked safe. The only thing that warned anyone was that the keyboard had been changed to Chinese.

Let's say you're in a club and your bouncer is the firewall. Zero trust means the bartender then still requires customers to see IDs. The bartender doesn't rely on checks and authentication from the bouncer or anyone else. That's because they may be allowing someone in the door based on different policies and conditions. Additionally, someone might not have even come through the bouncer's door. Maybe they came through the back patio. Therefore, we need to verify identity as close as possible to the point of access. And that's why the bartender will still ask for your ID.

What's Wrong With Implicit Trust?

Implicit trust is a problem. For example, the Colorado Department of Transportation ran into issues that resulted in ransomware and several weeks of outage. Take some time to look into this story by googling it.

Let's look at some trust assumptions:

- "It's only a temporary instance, so it doesn't need the usual security configurations."
- "Nobody will notice this instance."
- "We join everything to the internal domain, even if it's not internal, because that makes everything operate smoothly."

▶ "If you're part of the internal domain, we don't need to check you again."

We sometimes think it's only a temporary instance, so it doesn't need the usual security configurations. Or we might think that nobody will notice this instance. We can't make these assumptions.

Will network segmentation fix the problem? Yes and no. It depends on how granular it is. But the more granular it is, the more difficult is to maintain.

Another note on zero trust — it's not one tool or technology. It's a different way of thinking about resources both on and off our network.

How to Apply Zero Trust

There are different ways to apply zero trust.

First, think of the perimeter as being any place where you make access control decisions. For example, if you don't run your own network, then everything is potentially hostile. Move your security to the level that you can control.

Here's one example of a new and common perimeter: when people use the same applications for home and work. For example, if I log into my Google account at work, most companies don't care. However, if I'm logged in to my personal account, it becomes my employer's problem. The perimeter can be affected by which login information I put in.

There are three spots where zero trust can keep you safe: workforce, workload, and workplace. For example, in the workforce you want to know if the user is who they say they are. You want to know that they have the correct access and that their device is secure and trusted.

However, zero trust isn't just about users. When looking at workload, what applications are being used and what data is being communicated? And what data is passing between applications and how is it being secured? More and more encryption is used even within our networks.

And finally, let's look at the workplace. We may be using IoT, smart light bulbs, and other technologies during our working day. We may need to look at all devices that come inside with our employees. They may be vulnerable, so how do we segment them from the rest of our network?

Things Have Changed

In DevOps, you'll be responsible for more of this than you were in the past: when you're designing, coding, deploying and monitoring applications.

When looking at the chart below, consider how everything connects together. Depending on what talks to what, you'll have different security protocols and different security concerns.

You can look at all of these and see a number of opportunities to do authentication. And as you can see, the table isn't complete. We have some things to work out still.

For instance, there's one additional problem. Looking at the user role, see how many different authentication methods they must use to prove they are who they say they are. This results in cranky users that have to track all these different methods!

	TO DEVICES	TO APPS	TO NETWORKS	TO DATA	TO USERS
FROM DEVICES	SSH Certificates	Client-side TLS certificate Geofencing Fingerprinting	NAC	Encryption keys	
FROM APPS	Server-side TLS certificate	API Key		Encryption keys	Enhanced TLS certificates
FROM NETWORKS	802.1x certificate		Firewall rules		
FROM DATA	Hashes/ checksums	Hashes/ checksums			Hashes/ checksums
FROM USERS	User credentions 2FA Biometrics	User credentions 2FA Biometrics	User credentions 2FA	User credentions 2FA	Photo ID Handshake

Source: Sounil Yu

What to Pay Attention to With DevOps

With DevOps, you'll have to pay attention to impact and scale. Users in the DevOps world all have elevated privileges. They have access to a lot more than normal users would.

Additionally, you should look at inter-workload communications. You may not expect issues with one server talking to another server. However, when attackers attack, they take advantage of these lateral communications that no one thought to block. Yes, it's scary to whitelist everything that should have access to a system. And it may take time. But it will result in more security through zero trust.

Finally, realize that automation can both help and harm. It eases our workload, but it also drives to the lowest common denominator. So if you have to customize one particular thing for each application, you start giving everything the same general security policies and rules. Then you slip into a state where everything is talking to everything else. Policies are looser than they should be. Therefore, you should take the time to figure out granular security policies. Zero trust is not about making everything fall under the same policy.

So where will attackers move next? If we prevent lateral movement within networks, they'll probably switch to lateral movement between applications. You'll have to start thinking about securing your APIs more.

The Takeaway Message

One final thought to leave you with. Trust is neither binary nor permanent.

For example, your team may trust you to speak on a webinar. But they may not trust you to never break things. And even if they do trust you, that trust shouldn't be permanent.

Think about what you trust someone to do, what conditions need to be true, and for how long should this trust last. ∎

ABOUT THE PRESENTER

Wendy Nather is head of the Advisory CISO team at Duo Security (now Cisco). She was previously the Research Director at the Retail ISAC, as well as Research Director of the Information Security Practice at independent analyst firm 451 Research. Wendy led IT security for the EMEA region of the investment banking division of Swiss Bank Corporation (now UBS), and served as CISO of the Texas Education Agency. She speaks regularly on topics ranging from threat intelligence to identity and access management, risk analysis, incident response, data security, and societal and privacy issues. Wendy is co-author of *The Cloud Security Rules*, and was listed as one of *SC Magazine*'s Women in IT Security "Power Players" in 2014, as well as an "Influencer" in the Reboot Leadership Awards in 2018. You can find Wendy on Twitter at @WendyNather.

Summary provided by Sylvia Fronczak.

Go to bit.ly/2020addo-nather to watch the entire presentation.

CHAPTER 9

Managing a Remote DevOps Team

*presented by Mike Hansen,
Paula Thrasher, and Ross Clanton*

CHAPTER 9

Managing a Remote DevOps Team

Remote working experiences come in all shapes and sizes. When working on a remote DevOps team, you might encounter some unique challenges other than the usual communication technology failures. DevOps requires a high level of communication, and the transition from in-person teams to remote teams can leave people in shock. In this chapter, a panel of experts — Mike Hansen, Paula Thrasher, and Ross Clanton — discuss these challenges.

Comfort With Tools Does Not Mean Comfort With Working Remotely

Although your team might use tools like Microsoft Teams, Slack, and Zoom in the office, using them on remote teams brings more reliance on them. These tools become your connection to your world inside the organization. Things like virtual happy hours, video chat, and screen sharing help bring teams and people together.

Managing remote teams means using chat, according to Paula Thrasher. You can't just walk into someone's office or tap on a shoulder.

However, that doesn't mean privacy isn't an issue. With chat tools, text messaging, and even email, you've got to form good habits. Respect each other's privacy. As a reminder, most tools offer status settings so you can let others know that you're on lunch or "off the clock."

Onboarding in Remote Teams

Mike Hanson stresses being present and the value of having a good onboarding process. It's important to set the expectations, define boundaries, and make sure everyone knows their roles and responsibilities. This can keep people from burning out by keeping everyone focused.

It's up to leadership in the organization to set the standard. Leaders should keep the whole team in mind. So, what does this mean when you have team members in different time zones?

Whether you're a distributed company that's in an office or you're in a remote organization, time zone differences can cause issues with communications that delay projects. Being upfront about expectations and being aware of cultural differences can help ease the tensions that may form due to time zone differences (which may or may not also come with cultural differences).

Managing Distractions

When it comes to remote teams, most workers aren't working in a private office. This means distractions come with the territory — dogs, children, and all the unpredictable things that come with being in an environment not designed with productivity in mind.

Here are some tips you can use to minimize distractions:

▶ Establish a ritual.

▶ Work in a room with a door that locks.

▶ Have an "open door/closed door" policy.

▶ Communicate with others in your environment about calls and appointments.

While this list covers distractions in your environment, it might not cover distractions in your virtual space. This comes down to the same principles that you would apply while working in person, but with a lower-touch form of communication.

The tools help, but you also need clarity in your communication. You don't necessarily have visual radiators in your space. By visual radiators, we're talking about kanban boards, other people's screens, chatter in the room, and things like that. Those things are in the physical environment. So how do you translate those to the virtual environment?

Organizing Work for Productivity

Working remotely is a true test of how well your process works. If you can be productive in a remote environment, then you really know your team is productive.

In a way, it's also a true test of your leadership. Followers of a good leader will continue to put in their best efforts whether you're remote or not. So, working remotely is not only a test of your process, but it's also a great way to better understand your leadership skills.

But here's the crux of the matter, as it concerns productivity: how do we even measure it? We can't (and perhaps never should have) measure based on hours put in. We have to rely more on output. Results are the true measure of success and productivity.

The good news is that there's growing evidence that we're becoming more productive as more companies are fully remote than ever before. In one way, it enables collaboration between functional teams that have been physically separated in the office. This tighter communication can lead to better outcomes.

Other Concerns With Remote Teams

One topic that comes up with remote teams is security. Making sure you're set up with the right tools to either work outside the network or making sure your VPN can scale are two important considerations when going remote. You also have to give your people the tools they need or they'll turn to potentially insecure tools for things like communications and file sharing.

You'll want to integrate tools into the current environment. Remote tooling should work with the tools you use in the office rather than replace them. We need to be aware that mindset comes before tools. Ross Clanton says, put the right mindset first. If you have the right mindset for what your organization should be, all of the other things like process and tooling follow.

Tooling is there to support how you want your organization to function. If you need a hybrid environment, that's one consideration. Another factor is the extent to which your business network is distributed. These are just a few factors that might determine which tools you use.

Main Takeaways

To sum up this topic, we'll leave you with a few main takeaways from this conversation.

▶ Start with the right mindset.

▶ Respect boundaries.

▶ Give your organization secure tools.

▶ Use those tools to keep the mindset.

▶ Step up the quality of your communications.

▶ Be present, virtually.

▶ Be humans!

We're learning a lot as the world goes through so many transformations. One major transformation for so many people is going remote. We as a DevOps community are equipped technically to handle the changes, but we need to keep in mind the human aspects of these transformations. By aligning people and technology, we can make any transformation successful! ∎

ABOUT THE PRESENTERS

Paula Thrasher has led large digital and DevOps transformations as an executive for major companies in the Defense/Aerospace industry such as United Technologies (now Raytheon Technologies) and General Dynamics Information Technology (GDIT). She has transformed both inside the CIO organization, and also as a consultant to other US federal government agencies including NASA, FAA, USCIS, CBP, and Department of Navy. She has been recognized as an industry-wide leader in 2017 as DevOps Transformation Leader of the year by DevOps.com, and is known for her public speaking on digital topics. She spoke at the DevOps Enterprise Summit 2015, 2016, and 2017 conferences, AllDayDevOps, Keynoted RSA DevSecOps in 2018; has co-authored papers for IT Revolution's DevOps Enterprise Forum; and has been a guest on DevOps Café podcast.

Mike Hansen brings over 20 years experience building and leading product development organizations ranging from start-ups to the Fortune 100. He has been leading and scaling Sonatype's fully remote, product development engine for the past 8+ years from startup through growth stage. When not at work, you can often find him mountain biking, hiking and climbing the beautiful Colorado Rocky Mountains.

Ross Clanton has led multiple technology transformation and innovation initiatives across Verizon and Target. He is also an active collaborator in growing and strengthening the Enterprise DevOps community through his work with the DevOps Enterprise Forum, his podcast — The Goat Farm, and involvement in DevOps events nationally. Ross has had proven success establishing transformation strategy, driving culture change, scaling technology practices/skills through Dojo's, and driving platform strategies (Cloud, DevOps, API's) to improve technical excellence in some of the largest technology organizations in the world. His passion for DevOps stems not only from the fact that it improves business outcomes, but that it can also improve engagement and overall happiness of people working in technology.

Summary provided by Phil Vuollet.

Go to bit.ly/2020addo-thrasher *to watch the entire presentation.*

CHAPTER 10

The (Air) Force Awakens
From Kessel Run to the Moons of Bespin

presented by Lauren Knausenberger,
Enrique Oti, and Jeff McCoy

CHAPTER 10

The (Air) Force Awakens
From Kessel Run to the Moons of Bespin

auren Knausenberger, Enrique Oti, and Jeff McCoy have commandeered the term "agile AF"— it stands for Agile Air Force, in this instance. In this chapter, they detail exactly what this looks like.

What Does Moving Fast in Bureaucracy Mean?

Many people don't believe that the Department of Defense (DoD) can go agile. But when they see it, they're inspired. If the DoD can go agile, then anyone can.

First, Oti tells us a story about a project that starts back in Silicon Valley, where federal employees see their friends writing code and making millions of dollars. They wanted to know, "Why does the DoD software suck?" So Oti saw an opportunity and simply asked for resumes. He recruited six airmen and brought them to Pivotal Labs, where they learned to design and then code an app.

So what did they write for their first application? They looked at a problem that had previously been solved by a whiteboard. They looked at how to refuel planes in the air and how to plan and schedule this process. The traditional solution of using the whiteboard, with its flexibility and other benefits, was a formidable challenge to replace. They were tasked to build something better than that whiteboard! In four months they had built a successful application.

The Results for the Team

McCoy was one of the six airmen pulled in. His team, coming together from different backgrounds and organizations, had kept up their camaraderie and stayed in touch. Though there were conflicts and challenges, they grew stronger working together. Both the Air Force and the Pivotal Labs engineers learned from each other and grew their skills.

This application was a success not just because of the resulting product. The team overcame issues in a place where there were running jokes about how you can't write apps in the Air Force. They didn't have IDEs or tools. They had to write their code in Notepad and other simple editors, as everything was blocked for possible security threats. They were eventually able to get around that, and they credit modern DevOps tools for providing one of the biggest wins for Air Force application development.

Real, Continued Change

Along the way, the Air Force realized that they could theoretically be deploying code five times a day. The problem is, each time they deploy, they have to go through an authorization to operate (ATO) process, which takes as little as six months and as much as 18 months. So they worked to adopt commercial best practices to build a continuous ATO process.

Eventually, they got to a point where even people Knausenberger referred to as "supervillains" said that the Air Force was good with their continuous security integration. When the supervillains say you're good, you know you're good.

The first organization that tried this was the NGA, and the Air Force took advantage of their process. They took a release process down to 22 days, which then showed the opportunity to drop it down even more. They drove against the bureaucracy that they were seeing.

Why They Succeeded

Removing bureaucracy wasn't just done with pure force. They recruited the right people and created the right professional network to further the DevOps efforts. They realized that bringing everyone together to solve the problem would lead to better results.

Also, what they deployed worked, and that matters. You can't put together a massive plan for a massive budget: that would have not survived bureaucracy. So they simply built apps and shipped them. It was pretty on the front, fast and dirty on the back, and the customers loved it. They didn't build for scale at first and focused on getting something to their users. They focused on a minimum viable product in the early days.

Recently, they've strayed from MVPs and have become perfectionists at times. But lessons from the old days show them that there's value in quick and dirty to get something out in front of the users. Do something amazing and do it fast.

The Evolving Focus

Sometimes McCoy hears complaints about the architecture of some of the early systems like JigSaw, but he emphasizes their goal at the time. They were trying to get something out that works. They had a lot of people cycling through the product team. All of this results in less than ideal architecture. But it was still successful. The focus was on delivery.

By delivering something that users loved, fast, they showed that there was a better way: that you can build great systems within a bureaucracy. Sometimes you have to go fast to prove the value, and then people will change. You don't fight the bureaucracy; you revolutionize the organization by working with others to show them a new way.

Some of the focus has changed over time. For example, at SpaceCAMP and Platform One, some of the work now is hidden from the users. The work focuses on building a platform for other developers to help them move fast and deliver applications.

As you can see, the journey for the Air Force started with a quick and dirty drive that focused on solving problems for customers. They learned to prove their hypotheses and iterate on solutions. And now they're focusing on enabling other teams to do the same. ■

ABOUT THE PRESENTERS

Lauren Knausenberger recently joined the U.S. Air Force to drive innovation across the Department of Defense, speed adoption of emerging technologies, and create stronger partnerships between DoD, start-ups, and the venture community. Prior to joining the government, Lauren was founder and President of Accellint, Inc., a consulting firm specializing in solving problems of national security importance and investing in commercial technologies that could be applied to a government mission. An enthusiastic Angel investor, Lauren is active with NextGen Angels, has invested in emerging technology companies, such as Graphene Frontiers, and is now applying the VC model to the Air Force through Spark Tank, a DoD version of the Shark Tank television series. She holds an MBA from the Wharton School of Business, has served as an executive for a large defense contractor ,and has extensive experience supporting the intelligence community. Outside of work, Lauren enjoys traveling, trying new cuisine, and chasing two small children. She also recently founded a non-profit that encourages excellence in STEAM education.

Colonel Enrique Oti is the Commander of AFLCMC Detachment 12 (KESSEL RUN), where he is responsible for introducing commercial software development tools, methodologies, and culture into the Air Force. Under his portfolio, his team is modernizing the worldwide Air Operations Center enterprise, Targeting and GEOINT systems, F-35 maintenance systems, and a range of unit-level systems for command and control, and intelligence. Col Oti's operational deployments include Deputy J6, Joint Special Operations Task Force II, Brindisi Air Base, Italy, and Deputy J6 and then J35 planner, Combined Joint Special Operations Task Force Afghanistan, Bagram Air Base, Afghanistan.

Jeff McCoy is the CTO for Platform One, a group of nerds helping the DoD do DevSecOps right. They recently brought telework tools to tens-of-thousands of federal employees in a couple days, put Kubernetes on a fighter jet, are helping modernize major weapon systems and sport a Baby Yoda logo. Before Platform One, Jeff was the CTO of SpaceCAMP delivering modern software for Space Force and also helped create DDS's Rogue Squadron building counter-UAS software for special forces and North American defense. Jeff also really sucks at job interviews and was hired as the first Air Force UX designer for Kessel Run only to be reassigned as a lead engineer for the program the first day on the job.

Summary provided by Sylvia Fronczak.

Go to bit.ly/2020addo-knausenberger *to watch the entire presentation.*

CHAPTER 11

WTF is DevSecOps?

presented by Eliza May Austin

CHAPTER 11

WTF is DevSecOps?

I f you're a person working in security or software development, you've probably heard about DevSecOps before and wondered what it is or if it even works. Perhaps you're a DevSecOps practitioner and sometimes you're not sure about what you're doing. Is DevSecOps yet another tech buzzword? A trend?

So WTF is DevSecOps, anyway? Let's explore.

Is it Just a Trend?

If you go to any job board and type in "DevSecOps," you're immediately inundated with multiple listings with titles like "DevSecOps engineer," "DevSecOps practitioner," etc. In addition, many developers, pen testers, and security engineers are suddenly adding DevSecOps to their CVs in the hopes of getting opportunities in the field or even more compensation. So there's no doubt DevSecOps is trendy. Further, if you ask developers, they'll say, "It's great! We love it." And people who claim to have integrated DevSecOps are also big fans.

However, most security engineers have no clue what DevSecOps is.

By definition, DevSecOps is the practice of including security in the development process. It's mostly a philosophy or a process of doing things. Why would a philosophy/process have dedicated job listings?

Take the example of agile. As a security engineer, you might not necessarily practice agile, but you'd be able to work in an agile environment. Shouldn't it be the same with DevSecOps?

All this indicates that DevSecOps might be a trend more than anything else.

In theory, it's fantastic. Automating security? Security as code? All great ideas. However, in practice, it fails. Eliza polled multiple businesses in the UK and found that 88% of companies say they've already integrated DevSecOps or intend to integrate it in the next two to five years and yet, only 19% of these companies say that they're confident in their security integration.

There's no shortage of examples of apps that have gone live with vulnerabilities that were only discovered after shipping. What's more, this is after the apps supposedly went through the DevSecOps process.

So What's the Problem?

What's going on with these problems in DevSecOps shops? Well, at some companies, you might even find that the security team and the DevSecOps team are located in different cities. And that's a good indicator of where the problem might lie — in a lack of communication.

In fact, for the most part, it seems like the main reason DevSecOps might not be effective is that security teams are currently left out of the DevSecOps conversation.

At a glance, there are a couple of reasons this is the case:

1. Developers are expected to also be security experts. But that's ridiculous because no one expects security experts to also write code.
2. Those in the security community can find themselves outside of the DevSecOps conversation if they feel development process discussions are beneath them or if they find it difficult to admit to not knowing things.
3. There's a general assumption in the industry that DevSecOps is an alternative to security when really the two should be collaborative.
4. DevOps itself has outpaced traditional security controls. That leaves security to be handled separately.

So now what?

At the moment DevSecOps feels like this:

▶ A completely different department

▶ Something that does not involve me

▶ Something that's not my problem

▶ A meeting I may have to go to occasionally

▶ A concept people can't agree on

- ▶ A divisive issue

- ▶ Something in another building

- ▶ It's assumed what it is agreed upon

- ▶ Some automation thing the dev team does now

- ▶ An actual security risk

We'll have to work on communication for this to get better.

How Can We All Come Together?

In summary, DevSecOps is a great idea. But it will remain ineffective until we're all involved in the process. That means security engineers, DevSecOps teams, and developers working together.

Think of it as the same way a marketing team and an HR team works on social media for hiring collaboratively. If the HR team just posted jobs on social media without marketing or vice versa, the project wouldn't be successful.

The conclusion? If we could all collaborate on DevSecOps, we might have better results. ■

ABOUT THE PRESENTER

Eliza May Austin is the CEO of th4ts3cur1ty.company. She is also the Founder and Director of Ladies of London Hacking Society.

Summary provided by Elizabeth Kathure.

Go to bit.ly/2020addo-austin *to watch the entire presentation.*

CHAPTER 12

Kubernetes for Developers

presented by Hossam Barakat

CHAPTER 12

Kubernetes for Developers

We used to run multiple applications directly on the host server. Then we started using virtual machines for isolation. Containers allow us to further isolate the application and its dependencies on the host server(s).

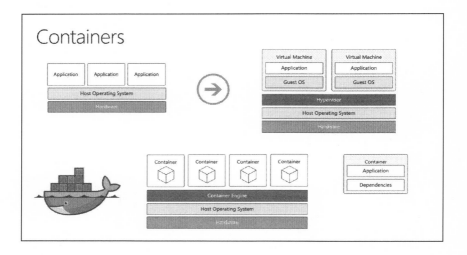

We can run more containers on the same host with less overhead from the guest OS that comes with virtual machines.

Scaling With Growth

Kubernetes helps to automate deploying, scaling, and managing many containers. It's not needed for a few containers. But it's the most popular container orchestration system. Kubernetes is architected as shown in this diagram.

Kubernetes Components

As you can see, Kubernetes is made up of several components.

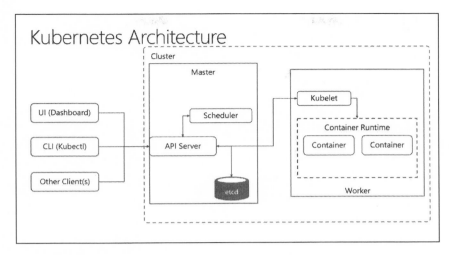

PODS

An application lives in a pod. To scale an application, we simply scale the pod. Pods are declared using a YAML doc and deployed using the CLI command: kubectl.

This pod definition is relatively simple. It contains a single container definition. The entire application can consist of several container definitions with more complex parameters than what you see here.

Pod

```
kind: Pod
apiVersion: v1
metadata:
  name: tasks-app
spec:
  containers:
  - name: tasks-app
    image: hossambarakat/tasklist
    ports:
      - containerPort: 80


    $ Kubectl apply -f pod.yaml
```

REPLICASETS

Pods are contained within replica sets for stability. If a pod is unhealthy, other pods in the replica set keep the application alive. Replica sets are also declared using YAML. A deployed replica set looks like the following:

Kubernetes assures that there will be three pods in the replica set shown above. You can easily scale the replica set up and down by changing the desired number of pods.

Deployment

A deployment contains one or many replica sets. The replica sets are versioned. It's this versioning that allows us to do rolling deployments and easy rollbacks. Deployments are defined in, you guessed it, YAML documents! And the deployment defines how you will roll out the new version of your application.

It takes a bit of a shift in your mental model. Releasing an application is a bit different using Kubernetes. There's no need to take the application offline. But it takes some planning to design the application changes in order to use this capability.

Service

A service connects pods using labels. This is important because pods are ephemeral, meaning that they might go away at any time. And when they do, the new pod that will replace it won't have the same IP address. So we can't connect pods using IP addresses. This is the importance of using a service!

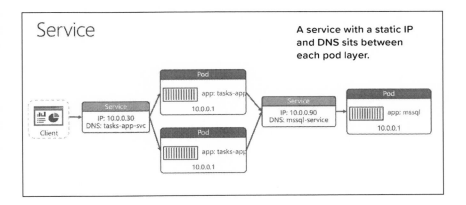

Volumes

Volumes are persistent storage devices that live beyond the life of a container. They can be used for the persistence of databases and other types of files that should live longer than any given pod. These volumes can be detached from one pod and mounted to another pod. Should the original pod go down, the volume can just be moved to the new one. This is how the data stored in volumes outlives any given pod or container.

Getting Started in the Cloud

There are several components to install and manage. If you start with a managed Kubernetes service, you won't have to spend the extra effort creating your own from scratch. Azure, GCP, and AWS each offer managed Kubernetes services, as do several other cloud providers.

Whether you're outgrowing your existing container environment or just curious, it's definitely worth checking out Kubernetes! ■

ABOUT THE PRESENTER

Hossam Barakat is a software consultant with over 13 years of experience delivering successful software projects. Specializing in Microservices, Serverless, Domain Driven Design, Agile and Lean software development, and Continuous Delivery. You can find Hossam on Twitter at @hossambarakat_.

Summary provided by Phil Vuollet.

Go to bit.ly/2020addo-barakat to watch the entire presentation.

OWASP Top 10 Overview

presented by Caroline Wong

CHAPTER 13

OWASP Top 10 Overview

O WASP is a very cool community dedicated to helping organizations build software that can be trusted. It came online in 2001 and was established as a non-profit in April of 2004.

Its core purpose is to be the thriving global community that drives visibility and evolution in the safety and security of the world's software. And its core values are to be open, innovative, global, and to have integrity.

There have been several iterations of the OWASP Top 10 since 2003. You can think of the Top 10 as basically a list of how not to get hacked. The official document provides information about determining your vulnerability, prevention strategies, examples, and testing strategies.

#1 Injection

Injection, loosely speaking, involves tricking systems into interpreting untrusted data as trusted commands (e.g. SQL injection).

To understand this, think of a file cabinet, and a robot that you tell to fetch files. "Robot, give me all files from 2019." With an injection attack, the attacker alters the instructions to the robot to "give me the files from 2019… and also all of the other files."

#2 Broken Authentication

Broken authentication happens when functions related to authentication are implemented incorrectly and can be exploited.

As an analogy, think of a Hide-A-Key that looks like a rock. Except, you don't actually hide the key very well at all. And then, a burglar just stumbles across the Hide-A-Key left, say, on your door mat, extracts the key, and uses it.

#3 Sensitive Data Exposure

In this scenario, sensitive data, such as PII, lacks adequate protection within a system.

Think of baby gates. With a baby gate, you limit the area to which the baby has access, allowing you to baby-proof a smaller area of the house. With sensitive data, put it somewhere special, and implement lots of security there.

#4 XXE (XML External Entities)

This is a category that has to do with over-extending trust, like category 1. In this case, the system puts too much trust in the information in an XML resource.

There is an XXE attack called "billion laughs," also known as an XML bomb. In this scenario, an attacker submits a small, harmless string, but it begins to expand into many more such strings, which do the same until the system experiences a denial of service.

#5 Broken Access Control

This happens when restrictions on what users are allowed to do are not properly enforced.

Imagine that you're at the airport and you present your boarding pass and ID to the gate agent. This person then authenticates you and allows you into the boarding area, which ultimately grants you access on the plane to your seat. You're not allowed to, say, wander into the cockpit, unless access control is broken.

#6 Security Misconfiguration

Security misconfiguration happens when you have manual, ad hoc, or incorrectly configured controls.

Many applications come insecure out of the box. For instance, imagine your phone. You have to go in and set up a passcode, fingerprint, or facial recognition. Without that, you have a de facto misconfiguration.

#7 Cross Site Scripting (XSS)

Cross site scripting allows attackers to execute scripts in the user's browser. It's another scenario where trusting data you shouldn't can cause issues.

For instance, consider a preschool where some children have severe food allergies. Parents can't send children to school with food. This effectively represents XSS-prevention, in that a parent can't create an issue for another child via their own child's lunch.

#8 Insecure Deserialization

This happens when an application receives hostile serialized objects and doesn't properly guard against them.

To understand insecure deserialization, imagine someone messing with a puzzle in the box. They're swapping out pieces, breaking them, and otherwise tampering. When another person then attempts to do the puzzle, it has been vandalized.

#9 Components with Known Vulnerabilities

This occurs when libraries and components run with the same trust-level as the application, and have known issues of their own.

Consider product recalls. The NHTSA allows you to search for all kinds of different recalls in automobiles. And, just as you'd want to keep yourself apprised of safety issues in things such as your car, you should do the same with your software.

#10 Insufficient Logging and Monitoring

Most security breaches are not discovered by the organization that has been breached, but rather by its users. Insufficient logging and monitoring means that the organization is not taking enough steps to become aware of breaches.

While logging is important, logging without monitoring is useless. consider the monkey monitoring the screens in *Toy Story 3*. To make an escape, the characters disable the monitoring monkey's ability to notify anyone about what's happening. So the escape is logged, but the alert mechanism (the monkey) doesn't work, meaning there is effectively no monitoring.

This is the OWASP Top 10 as they stand today. Expect this list to change. ∎

ABOUT THE PRESENTER

Caroline Wong is the Chief Security Strategist at Cobalt.io. Her close and practical information security knowledge stems from broad experience as a Cigital consultant, a Symantec product manager, and day-to-day leadership roles at eBay and Zynga. She is a well-known thought leader and has contributed content to LinkedIn Learning and Forbes. Caroline has been featured in multiple Women in IT Security issues of *SC Magazine* and was named one of the Top Women in Cloud by CloudNOW. She received a Women of Influence Award in the One to Watch category and authored the popular textbook *Security Metrics: A Beginner's Guide*, published by McGraw-Hill. Caroline graduated from U.C. Berkeley with a B.S. in Electrical Engineering and Computer Sciences and holds a certificate in Finance and Accounting from Stanford University Graduate School of Business. Caroline's courses on LinkedIn Learning provide more detail about the OWASP Top 10. You can find Caroline on Twitter at @CarolineWMWong.

Summary provided by Erik Dietrich.

Go to bit.ly/2020addo-wong2 to watch the entire presentation.

CHAPTER 14

DevOps Assurance With OWASP SAMM

presented by Seba Deleersnyder

CHAPTER 14

DevOps Assurance With OWASP SAMM

We're going to discuss OWASP. More specifically, we'll focus on SAMM and how it pairs with DevOps. If you're not familiar with OWASP or SAMM v2 (software assurance maturity model), everything can be found at owasp.org, along with some of the flagship projects.

There are several DevOps maturity models; however, they are exclusively for DevOps. SAMM v2 aims to add security to the development lifecycle, in other words, it adds a secured layer to the development operations.

Useful for organizations small or big, SAMM adds assurance to the DevOps process.

In this chapter, you'll be introduced to SAMM v2 and walked through the new features added in this version of the model, how it integrates into the DevOps workflow, and how it differentiates itself from other maturity models.

Why Do I Need a Maturity Model?

Before we get ahead of ourselves, you might be wondering why you need a maturity model.

Adding a security layer to the development lifecycle isn't easy. A maturity model like SAMM helps you with this by adding security levels in an iterative way, rather than in a "big bang" approach. SAMM is something you need to adapt to your development process. It's not a silver bullet for your day-to-day operation processes, and it must be adapted to your unique development target.

A good maturity model provides enough details to the users while being simple, well-defined, and measurable.

What's SAMM All About?

SAMM is, fundamentally, a set of security practices organized in five main business functions:

1. Governance

2. Design

3. Implementation

4. Verification

5. Operations

Previously familiar users will see a new item: the implementation security practice. This includes:

▶ Secure build

▶ Secure deployment

▶ Defect management

The new version incorporates these features given their increase in importance over the past years.

Defect Management

Just for the sake of time, we're going to focus on just one of the new security practices: defect management.

SAMM v2 is built following three levels of maturity and two streams, which we can easily compare with similar DevOps models. Maturity levels 1 through 3 are similar to what in other models are known as crawling, walking, and running. A simplified way to think through the different layers is:

▶ Maturity 1 means tracking all bugs and defects.

▶ Reaching maturity 2 would require fixing the errors.

▶ As the development process grows, we'd need to implement maturity 3, which includes adding agreements and compliances.

As with other DevOps practices, it's not a goal for every organization to reach maturity 3. Moreover, adapting the model or deciding which phases to integrate will depend on what suits your development operation. Several factors, like how quickly you move across different maturity levels, will have an impact on the final maturity level.

How Do We Get Started?

To get started, we first need to assess the state of the development operation. A very straightforward tool we've included as part of the new release is a simple spreadsheet that's designed to feel like an interview. It'll measure your operations in terms of streams and maturity levels. Each level has questions linked to a security activity.

In the end, the tool provides a maturity score with color-coded results split by business function. It also provides the ability to add a roadmap with guidance on what to do next with security activities.

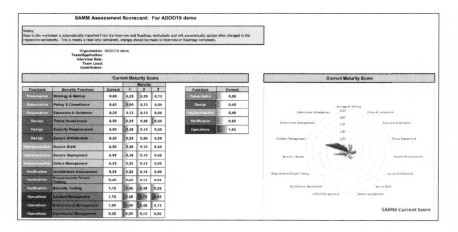

It's truly an educational tool for your organization.

Start Applying SAMM

If you're not familiar with DevOps, a book called *The Phoenix Project* is a great place to start learning.

In essence, DevOps provide a list of common workflows within your development team to create value for your organization. Ideally, using the right model provides instant feedback cycles and a shared culture on how to improve as a team.

Adding security to the DevOps workflow should be part of the organization's culture. The process consists of three steps:

▶ Awareness training

- ▶ Security champions
- ▶ Security culture

Once your team goes through those, you include security practices to your typical DevOps cycle.

Should you need help with that, OWASP provides guidance, which is publicly available, in order to better orient people on where to start. Whether the model is agnostic or not, the process is very collaborative, and there's plenty of help available.

Visiting owaspsamm.org provides a community and living documentation. It mostly highlights the past version (v1.5), however, it's still relevant and worthwhile to browse the website.

By following a continuous integration process, the SAMM creators are able to iterate quickly and distribute information a lot faster. The information on the website is also broken down in easy to manage pieces.

What's Next?

After SAMM v2, the improvements and iterations to the model can be applied faster, and, of course, there's a bigger community willing to help collaboratively. More OWASP references are on the way, along with more consistent guidance. People are now able to use the toolbox spreadsheet discussed above. Additionally, they'll include it as part of the website so that benchmarks can be provided.

Collaborating is easy through the OWASP Slack channel as well as in GitHub. You're also free to join the mailing list. You'll receive updates occasionally.

The SAMM v2 project is not a one-man show. It's a collaborative effort from an international team. By all means, everyone is welcome to join or sponsor the project. ■

ABOUT THE PRESENTER

Seba Deleersnyder is co-founder, CEO of Toreon and a proponent of application security as a holistic endeavor. He started the Belgian OWASP chapter, was a member of the OWASP Foundation Board and performed several public presentations on Application Security. Seba also co-organized the yearly security & hacker BruCON conference and trainings in Belgium. With a background in development and many years of experience in security, he has trained countless developers to create software more securely. He has led OWASP projects such as OWASP SAMM, thereby truly making the world a little bit safer. Now he is adapting application security models to the evolving field of DevOps and is also focused on bringing Threat Modeling to a wider audience. You can find Seba on Twitter at @sebadele.

Summary provided by Guillermo Salazar.

Go to bit.ly/2020addo-deleersnyder *to watch the entire presentation.*

Being Budget Conscious in a Continuously Automated World

presented by Tim Davis

CHAPTER 15

Being Budget Conscious in a Continuously Automated World

One way to bring more business alignment with IT in DevOps is through continuous verification with things like security and budgets. Oftentimes these things are an afterthought until the last minute, but we can bring them into the pipeline and continuously think about them as we deliver software.

What Is Continuous Verification?

Continuous verification is the weaving of budget and other concerns directly into our DevOps pipeline.

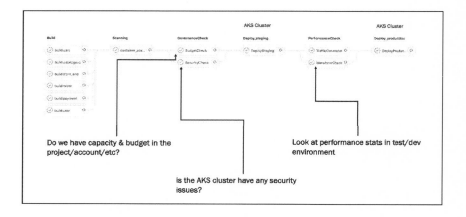

In the public cloud, you can quickly find yourself spending more money than you thought you were. It's so easy to purchase new services that overspending can sneak up on you. Traditionally, this can snake up through the finance department, resulting in you getting flooded with a slew of angry emails.

Instead, we can keep an eye on things, ensuring we're consistently within budget. There are many tools that can help us do this. CloudHealth from

VMWare is great for cost. Tools like Clair and SecureState help us with security and compliance.

Why Should it Be CI/CD/CV?

It's extremely important to be doing these verifications inside your pipeline because it keeps it on the top of your mind. At all times, you're preventing these issues from becoming large ones.

Demo of Continuous Verification

There is a great demo of continuous verification that you can find at gitlab.com/vtimd/addo-script.

You can see, through GitLab, both a budget and security check. Later in the pipeline, you can see a traffic check to ensure performance is stable. In the demo, you can see that the Wavefront performance check failed.

The great part here is that this pipeline lets us fail faster. If we run out of budget or don't meet performance needs, we cancel that pipeline. We don't continue to push and overspend.

In the demo, the entire pipeline is configured through one file. It is easy to turn off and on parts of the pipeline to speed it up and understand how it works.

The demo uses a ch-gitlab-script.py in Python that does most of the heavy lifting. The deployment config uses much for this script's functions to run each step in the pipeline.

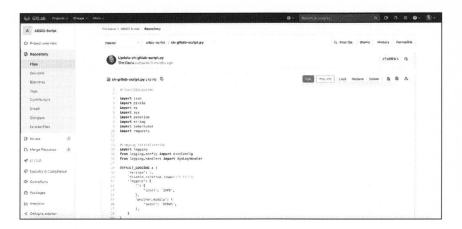

The scripts that run are neither VMWare- nor GitLab-proprietary. Anyone can do such scripting. Note also how things like "Bill Tokens" and other variables are parameterized. We want to inject these into the scripts and not hardcode them, as we want to be able to run this across environments and keep sensitive information secure.

Conclusion

To summarize, doing continual verification is not technically hard. You don't have to familiarize yourself with large amounts of new tools, either. You can do this with many of the tools you're already familiar with. But the value you get from continually verifying budget, security, and performance is immeasurable. ∎

ABOUT THE PRESENTER

Tim Davis is a Cloud Advocate at VMware where he focuses on public cloud operations and cloud-native applications. He provides consulting guidance to a wide range of customers on these topics and provides a bridge between customers and product teams at VMware. He also works to evangelize native cloud usage, including AWS / Azure / GCP. Prior to his current role, he was a Specialist Systems Engineer focused on VMware's Networking and Security product line. Before VMware, Tim worked as a Consultant and VMware Architect at Dell Services, working for one of the largest contracts they held at the time. His background is in operations / management, and architecture. He holds numerous industry certifications, including VMware and Amazon Web Services. You can find Tim on Twitter at @vtimd.

Summary provided by Mark Henke.

Go to bit.ly/2020addo-timdavis to watch the entire presentation.

OWASP Juice Shop
The Ultimate All Vuln WebApp

presented by Björn Kimminich

CHAPTER 16

OWASP Juice Shop
The Ultimate All Vuln WebApp

A lot of people who want to become (ethical!) hackers learn whatever they can from videos, blogs, and books. And after that, they're in a state of doubt — they aren't sure if they can actually hack something.

Once you have theoretical knowledge, you need practical experience. And obviously, you can't practice hacking on some random website that's out there because that's illegal and will get you in trouble.

That's where OWASP Juice Shop comes in. It's a web application that looks like any other shopping website, but it's designed to be vulnerable on purpose so people can practice hacking.

What Does Juice Shop Look Like to an Ordinary Visitor?

Once you install Juice Shop and start using it, it's just like any other shopping website. This site lets you order juice.

You see a menu with a list of juices that you can order, along with their prices. There's a button that lets you add the juice to the basket. In the basket page, you can see all the juices you've chosen, and you can place the order.

You can consider this appearance as a "front" for the main reason this application was built. Now, let's find out what that actually is.

What Does Juice Shop Look Like to a Hacker?

Juice Shop is an application filled with more than 88 web vulnerabilities. Once you install it and use it from a hacker's perspective, you'll see that there are various weak points where you can hack the application.

One of the best things about Juice Shop is that it not only lets you hack the application but also notifies you when you've succeeded! You also have a scoreboard where you can see the list of exploits you've completed and the ones you should work on.

You'll find six difficulty levels, from beginner to expert. So it doesn't matter if you've just started hacking or if you've been into it for some time now: Juice Shop will still be fun.

What if you've had enough of hacking that day and want to take a break? No problem. Juice Shop will save your status. So the next time you log in, all the previous hacks you've completed will be marked, and you don't have to do them all over again.

What's Good About Juice Shop?

A lot of people who want to practice hacking are beginners. So Juice Shop also has an interactive tutor called a "hacking instructor" that'll help you figure out what to do.

One thing that may interest you as a hacker is the Capture the Flag (CTF) challenge. You can also use Juice Shop in the CTF mode by making some changes to the configuration.

CTF mode is great because you can set up Juice Shop with other CTF servers. Then you'll have to create a logic to generate flags. In this case, you can hand out a separate instance of Juice Shop to each participant. (You can learn more about CTF here.)

If you get bored with how Juice Shop looks, you have an option to customize it. This comes in handy when you want to make the application look like it belongs to a particular domain.

Juice Shop allows you to have test automations. You can use application programming interfaces to test if the challenges work.

The Tech Side of Juice Shop

Juice Shop uses AngularJS for the front end and NodeJS and Express framework for backend development.

It uses Sequelize Database for login operations. It also has SQLite and an in-memory NoSQL database. This allows it to run on a single docker container, which helps keep things simple.

The DevOps is almost fully automated, with lint tests, end-to-end testing, smoke testing, and so on. Only the release part is manual.

INSTALLING JUICE SHOP

You can run Juice Shop on Docker, Vagrant, and various cloud platforms. You can read more about the run options at bkimminich.gitbooks.io/pwning-owasp-juice-shop/content/part1/customization.html.

And if you're interested, all you have to do is go to the Juice Shop site at owasp.org/www-project-juice-shop. ■

ABOUT THE PRESENTER

Björn Kimminich is the project leader of the OWASP Juice Shop and a board member for the German OWASP chapter.

Summary provided by Omkar Hiremath.

Go to bit.ly/2020addo-kimminich to watch the entire presentation.

CHAPTER 17

There's No Nice Way to Say This

Your DevOps Has Gone Horribly Wrong

presented by Kalle Sirkesalo

CHAPTER 17

There's No Nice Way to Say This
Your DevOps Has Gone Horribly Wrong

DevOps is not about the tools. Nor is it about the number of people working on any given thing. Adding people doesn't mean delivering faster. You've got to measure what matters.

Sources of Problems

Using DevOps practices can make it easy to add environments as the team grows. However, each environment adds to the pool of technical debt. All of the tools can be in place and you can have proper Gitflow branches, CI/CD, and automated testing. Even though everything is technically correct, organizations can have problems delivering.

What Kalle is getting at here is that you need more than just the cool tools to succeed. And, in some cases, the tools can compound existing problems, making things worse instead of better.

Long-Running Branches

One source of trouble — a practice smell if you will — is long-running branches. These branches become difficult to merge and difficult to test. But this is just a symptom of a deeper problem. If something like having too many environments is blocking your deployment, you may end up with long-running branches. Merging your changes into a branch for each of these environments invites difficult merges. You'll have to merge over and over again — once per environment branch.

Different Processes

Another compounding factor of making life difficult for developers, ops, and the business alike is having teams that operate under different processes. Misaligned hierarchies can create political and communication barriers that you must progress past.

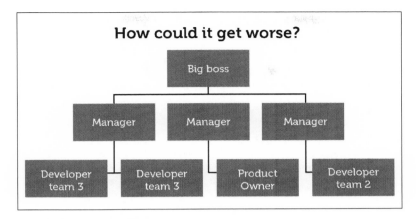

In this case, the product owner gets overridden by development managers on both sides. This hierarchy also creates an "up-and-over" communications path between teams. That in turn introduces communications delays and other related issues.

DevOps Is No Guarantee

DevOps is simply a way to enable teams to go faster. However, it doesn't guarantee this desirable outcome. Communication is still extremely important. It may be hard to talk about why, though. Teams may have excuses like they don't have time to do the important things such as prioritizing the backlog, asking why things need to be done, and refactoring code to make it more readable.

Even in a DevOps enabled environment, you still need planning. Scrum framework practices such as sprint goals, backlog grooming, sprint scoping, and communication are just as important to moving fast as tools that enable speed.

Achieving the goals of speed and accuracy is really all about collaborating. Collaboration and communication enable teams to be truly successful. No matter what technologies and processes you have in place, don't forget the all-important people aspect! ∎

ABOUT THE PRESENTER

Kalle Sirkesalo is the Platform Director at Eficode. With his strong track record in IT and DevOps, he has helped many small and large companies to build, automate, and scale their DevOps environments. Kalle describes himself as a fast learner workaholic, driven by self-improvement. You can find Kalle on Twitter at @Failattu.

Summary provided by Phil Vuollet.

Go to bit.ly/2020addo-sirkesalo to watch the entire presentation.

CHAPTER 18

Managing DevOps Teams
Staying Alive

presented by Marc Cluet

CHAPTER 18

Managing DevOps Teams
Staying Alive

D evOps speeds up development and allows faster results. However, most organizations struggle with its adoption. In this chapter, you'll learn about managing DevOps teams and get advice on conducting DevOps transformations at organizations.

Now, first things first. Let's establish some common ground.

What's DevOps About After All?

DevOps isn't only a bunch of tools to plan, develop, deploy, operate, and get feedback about software products. DevOps is more of a cultural view toward software development. Therefore, keep in mind the C of Culture in the five values (CALMS) of DevOps that follow:

▶ **C**ulture. DevOps is about people, processes, and using the right tools to support people in carrying out processes.

▶ **A**utomation. Whenever possible, optimize tasks and processes by writing automation scripts.

▶ **L**ean. Instead of building a car, start by building a bike. Then move on with an iterative and incremental approach. As a result, you'll end up with the car.

▶ **M**easurement. Use metrics to extract relevant and valuable conclusions.

▶ Sharing. Knowledge transfer activities are very important, as well as documentation.

In short, DevOps is optimizing and learning.

▶ **Optimizing.** Optimize the engineering by means of automation and a lean spirit.

▶ **Learning.** Learn from past outcomes — whether they were successful or not —through the sharing and measurement values in CALMS.

In case you already have a DevOps team in place, it's time to do things right and follow DevOps patterns.

Follow DevOps Patterns

There are four main DevOps patterns you should implement:

- **Increase communication.** Communication must take place not only within each team, but also across teams.

- **Organize brown bag sessions.** Ensure that knowledge transfers happen naturally and regularly, in a more formal way. For instance, organize brown bag sessions weekly or twice a week.

- **Pair programming.** At least two engineers sit next to each other and work together on solving the same problem. Together they produce better outcomes in a shorter period of time. Measure the number of successful deployments to production and the speed of delivery to prove value.

- **Feed a blameless culture.** Embrace mistakes as soon as they occur. Don't avoid them! They're an inevitable part of human nature and the way to learn and evolve. Make team members comfortable discussing failure as a team and find a solution that everybody agrees on.

Besides following DevOps patterns, you need to foster a DevOps culture, and that starts with people.

What Does a DevOps Manager Do?

A DevOps manager reinforces the team as a group and enables the teams to make the right decisions. They are a facilitator and responsible for delivery. But that's only a small slice of the melon. A DevOps manager must also do the following:

- **Inspire.** Expose the team to new technologies. Guarantee that the team's aware of the business vision and their contribution to it.

- **Protect.** Ensure that the focus of the team is on the tasks at hand. Do whatever it takes to protect the team from interference, either from members of other teams or business stakeholders.

- **Nurture.** Enable team members to make decisions and trust them to do it.

- **Celebrate success.** Celebrate the accomplishments of both individual team members and the team as a whole.

▶ **Challenge ideas.** Use positive criticism to lead team members to think. Prepare them for handling future problems with high quality solutions.

▶ **Communicate effectively with business stakeholders.** Have a clear and well-defined roadmap that they understand. Guarantee that what your team's work is in line with business practices and standards. Show value, especially to the final customer, by using metrics.

If your organization isn't a DevOps organization, then what can you do to achieve that?

Transforming Your Organization Into a DevOps Organization

Transformation implies change. And any change in an organization creates tension between people, processes, and tools. For instance, a sudden change in the way people interact creates a lot of tension on processes and tools. Tension creates pain and makes business stakeholders step away from transformation. So, don't make changes too quickly or without prior notice.

Start by using DevOps as a bridge between your Dev and Ops silos.

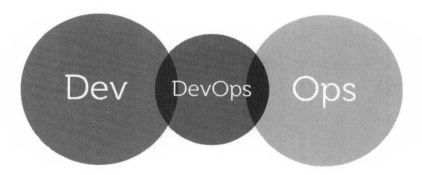

Then, break down the walls between Dev and Ops so they start working together.

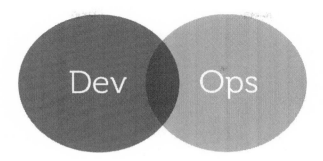

Progressively increase collaboration between your Dev and Ops teams until they are working in sync as a single DevOps team.

When transforming your organization into a DevOps organization, remember that change takes time. Invest in the right people to build a strong DevOps culture, and you'll get there.

Patience + Practice = Payoff

To sum up, building a DevOps team takes time. Nevertheless, the benefit of Dev and Ops teams working together pays off. In the meantime, just keep going and keep measuring change until the benefit becomes visible. ∎

ABOUT THE PRESENTER

Marc Cluet is the Co-Founder at Ukon Cherry, a London based consultancy specialising in DevOps. Marc has over 21 years of experience in the Industry, including companies like Rackspace, Canonical, Trainline, DevOpsGroup, Nationwide Building Society and several startups across five different countries. Marc has also spoken in some of the most prestigious conferences including FOSDEM, LISA, OpenStack Summit, UDS, Puppetconf and several meetups. Marc also is one of the organisers of London DevOps which is the second biggest DevOps meetup in the world. Marc has contributed code to several projects including Puppet, mcollective, Juju, cloud-init and helped create MAAS. Marc loves solving complex infrastructure problems and applying solid and repeatable solutions, he is also an expert in building up agile engineering teams. You can find Mark on Twitter at @lynxman.

Summary provided by Sofia Azevedo.

Go to bit.ly/2020addo-cluet2 to watch the entire presentation.

The World Bank Group's Cloud Journey With DevSecOps

presented by William Zhang, Andy Gao, and Srini Kasturi

CHAPTER 19

The World Bank Group's Cloud Journey With DevSecOps

As an overview, the World Bank Group is made up of several organizations that work towards ending extreme poverty across the world and boosting shared prosperity. They work on many fronts, including water and transportation improvements. Much of their work includes processing financial transactions and handling sensitive data, and they therefore saw a need to move towards DevSecOps.

To begin the DevSecOps journey, they first moved to SaaS solutions, like Office 365 and SharePoint Online. They then began including other SaaS solutions like Saba for training. And then finally, they moved into infrastructure-as-a-service from providers like AWS and Microsoft Azure.

Why was this necessary? Well, previously they needed to wait for months if not years to get necessary upgrades to their software and infrastructure. Cloud-based platforms gave them the agility they needed to stay ahead. Now when the service provider has an update, it can easily be upgraded in their systems.

Next up, they needed to start looking at applications, in addition to their infrastructure and cloud software. So where did they start on the application side? Back around 2008 or 2009, the World Bank Group embraced the idea that security fix can cost you more money when it's done at the end of the SDLC, like with a typical waterfall model.

The traditional approach wouldn't work. Security was looked at near the end. Because of that, there's always a desire to shift left and bring security checks earlier in the life cycle.

The business increased the need to shift left through their cloud-based expectations, where upgrades and patches occurred not in months or years but in weeks, days, or even hours!

They would have to align with a different approach.

A Journey to Automated Testing

To start off, they identified what manual testing occurred and where they could replace it with automated testing. The longer the automated testing took or the larger the volume of testing required, the more important it could be to automate.

For example, a routine review of reports would require a lot of manual reviews, but they'd only require action in certain situations. The most significant risk decisions that took time required automation.

They also had to look at scalability and quality. For example, OWASP Zap could run millions of tests. However, that would reduce cycle time. So they needed to prioritize tests based on what had the most business value.

Agile Approach to Security — Act I

To meet the demands of business and security, they took up a phased approach to pave their way to automated cloud security testing.

In the first phase, they focused on the bread and butter of services. Then they expanded that to the cloud-based services.

Next, once they selected a service, they had to decide what to automate. They had to look at what made sense from an architecture standpoint.

And they also had to answer a question — should they go completely left? Or should they create a loosely coupled model that can handle the churn that's going on in the World Bank Group?

They chose to not go completely left and instead used risk-based decision making to determine what changes to make first.

With this risk-based decision making, they determined how to budget in exemptions as well as provisions. Additionally, they looked at all the decisions being made and found that those decisions needed to be automated. And now they have 400 or so security decisions being made automatically.

And here's another learning from their journey: they found out that security also required operational support. This was no longer an 8–5 job. The DevSecOps team needed to provide extended support to assist with security issues around the clock. And finally, they realized that a better onboarding process would assist development teams to improve their security process.

Agile Approach to Security — Act II

For Act II, the World Bank group sought to look at infrastructure through infrastructure-as-code. They looked at the tools available in AWS to codify their security control tools.

As part of this, they combined the security stack with the application stack using AWS Service Catalog.

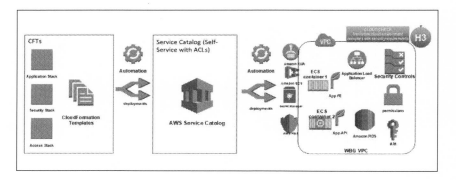

The security stack involves security and controls at the server level. The access stack includes ACL controls for applications. They then combined this to put them together in the service catalog. The AWS service catalog provided a guardrail, allowing others with one API call to get the data they needed securely.

Acts I and II Together

After reviewing Act I and Act II, the World Bank Group looked at security-as-code. This codifies security controls and builds controls verification into DevSecOps tools and practices.

So what does the pipeline look like? One thing the World Bank Group recommends is to make sure that your pipeline matches your business process. Their pipeline includes several safeguards for improved security.

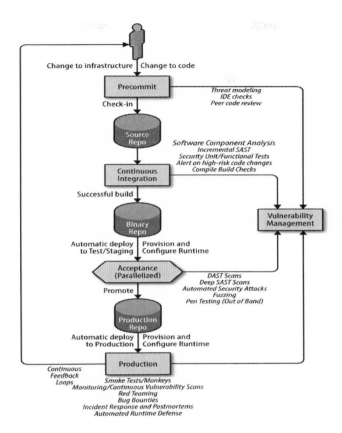

Next Steps

Next, the World Bank Group will move towards pipeline-as-code, as well as security-as-code for SaaS platforms. They'll also look at additional security hooks based on industry best practices.

And finally, they'll be looking at robotics process automation, machine learning, and natural language processing for additional security improvements. ■

ABOUT THE PRESENTERS

Dr. Zhijun (William) Zhang is the lead information security architect at The World Bank Group, where his team is responsible for security architecture design and assessment of all business solutions. William is a technology enthusiast and an active participant of the World Bank Group's Innovation Lab activities, including many financial service use cases. Before joining the World Bank Group, William worked at The Vanguard Group, a large financial service organization in the US, in various capacities, including user experience design, emerging technology research, system architecture, and information security. William received his bachelor's and master's degrees in computer science from Peking University, and Ph.D. in computer science from the University of Maryland.

Summary provided by Sylvia Fronczak.

Go to bit.ly/2020addo-zhang *to watch the entire presentation.*

Breaking Bad
DevOpsSec to DevSecOps

presented by Sean Davis

CHAPTER 20

Breaking Bad
DevOpsSec to DevSecOps

I n this chapter, you'll be guided through DevSecOps from a holistic view, using the story of *Breaking Bad* as the basis for exploration. Keep an open mind while we kick things off. And get ready for some *Breaking Bad* spoilers!

Characters

Let's start off with Walter. He's a seasoned pro. He's seen trends come and go, so he's a bit skeptical. He wants to transform DevOpsSec to DevSecOps.

Jesse is our code slinger and has seen it all. He loves a challenge and has street cred.

Todd represents security. He's not the smartest guy in the room, but makes up for it with ingenuity and creativity. He's never met a website he can't hack.

Then Lydia is operations, and she's always on. She's about the uptime. And she's constantly in planning mode.

Finally, Saul is the voice of the businessman: clever, charismatic, and able to sell his way into and out of anything.

A Word on DevSecOps and the Periodic Table of DevOps

Many people say that if you're doing DevOps, security should be built in. It should, but security didn't have a seat at the table when DevOps came about. However, now all three have a seat at the table. All three have been integrated and aligned at each step to deliver value.

DevSecOps is more like DevOps 2.0. But it doesn't matter what you call it. It matters what you do with it.

When you look at everything in play in the Periodic Table of DevOps, it's a huge table of tools.

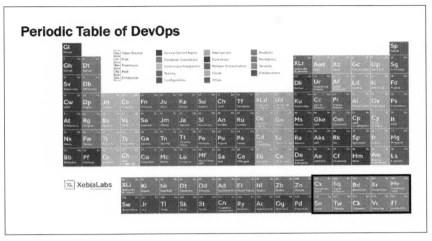

Image courtesy of XebiaLabs.

But now let's look at the security part of the table. It's off in the bottom right corner by itself, small and segregated. What do you think that means from a perception standpoint? How do companies view security and how it fits into the DevOps world?

Next let's look at DevOpsSec formula for mayhem.

We've got tools added in, with CD and monitoring, JIRA, and all the other hot new tools.

Security is again a smaller piece of the picture, and it's off to the side. There we've got GRC, risk, and other tools. But just because it's off to the side doesn't mean we shouldn't worry about it.

The Story Continues

So let's continue with Walter. They've had a recent breach and security has been made the focus. However, security once again was just bolted on at the end. Walter realizes that we can't have that. It can't just be a handoff between steps in the bigger picture.

Walter knows he has things that need to be done. He sees that we have operations, security, development, and business. So what does he do? Whatever is necessary.

To start, he talks to the developers. They know their stuff and don't want people encroaching on their turf. When they're not aligned with others, everyone is going to lose. They make a lot of quick decisions, and security isn't always top of mind.

So Walter works with Todd to figure out how to make their development operation move faster. He then embeds Todd with the developers. They can share the challenges each team is working through and open the lines of communication. Things start moving in the right direction.

Unfortunately, the business comes in and throws unreasonable deadlines at the teams. And everything seems to get in the way of delivering value. Security is again stepping in to slow things down.

Next, Walter reaches out to operations. He has to partner with Lydia here. With the goal of determining how operations and security interact, he finds that operations loves data. And they're also incentivized differently. They focus on automation, stability, monitoring, and alerting. Walter realizes that ops and devs need to find a common incentive that doesn't cause friction between the teams. And then when you pull in security, it adds additional friction.

So Walter and Todd are making progress. They're starting discussions with developers earlier and teaching them threat modeling. They're showing the devs what operations and security need to be successful. Communication is improving between all these teams.

But Then, Trouble

Then disaster strikes. Security is blamed; operations takes a hit. Everyone is confused and no one understands who's responsible for what.

So we realize that security being left out causes a lot of issues. They start tightening the screws and reinforcing once again.

But developers try to find workarounds so they can still go fast. And in turn, security pushes more demands and red tape onto the dev team. Everyone becomes frustrated. Walter realizes the problem — security is always lagging behind.

It's not security's fault. They're forced to react. So what can we do?

Saul to the Rescue... ?

Walter is on the hunt to find Saul. And when he finally finds Saul, Saul throws money at the problem.

Walter brings everyone together to build a new plan. A reorganization develops, bringing together a tiger team. With shiny new tools and equipment, energy is high.

Everyone is working to make this a success. Alliances form, and some teams find success. However, security is still not involved. Some things are better, but other things are still off.

Devs appreciate the automated testing from security, but then they're inundated with security tasks in the backlog. Operations and SRE start a turf war over how to support the product. Things are slowing down again.

Saul becomes frustrated with Lydia. He supplied the funds. Where are the benefits?

And Lydia focuses again on stability, slowing releases down and preventing new features from getting out. The cycle begins again.

Customers are irate. No one understands what's gone wrong. We're still not getting the difference that we want.

What Were the Mistakes?

Let's look at Walter's mistakes and how the outcome could be changed.

First, Walter missed team alignment with business goals and security needs. Everyone needs to be aware of what needs to be fixed first.

Next, Walter missed a key fact: blameless operations could have prevented outages. Operations could have come in and worked with developers to understand how each team works and what each team should focus on.

And then, when Walter identified that devs were working around security to deliver value, he still missed key opportunities to build alignment in all the teams.

When the business brought in big funds to solve the problem, Walter needed to the team to not just buy in. He needed to keep them engaged. And he needed to train the other teams on security concerns so it wasn't just security's torch to carry.

And finally, Walter missed a key focus on the culture shift. He needed to work to bring all the teams into alignment and improve communication.

So don't be like Walter. Though he made a lot of strides in getting everyone involved, it could have been different, and the tragic ending could have been prevented. ■

ABOUT THE PRESENTER

Sean Davis is an IT veteran with almost 20 years of experience covering every realm of IT. Approaching problems with childlike wonder, leveraging a library of skills as a polyglot and solving the unsolvable is the day-to-day. His current primary areas of expertise are around DevOps, Agile Coaching, Life Coaching, and Business Transformation. He loves to meet people, share knowledge and help others grow. You can find Sean on Twitter at @seanasaservice.

Summary provided by Sylvia Fronczak.

Go to bit.ly/2020addo-seandavis to watch the entire presentation.

Holding the Industry Accountable

presented by Chris Roberts

CHAPTER 21

Holding the Industry Accountable

We're going to have a conversation about holding our feet to the fire. We're going to break down what's going on in the industry and why we should care about it. Then we'll talk about what we should change, as well as why we should change it.

First, Why Are We Failing?

Going back to childhood, we were told not to touch a hot kettle on the stove. But what did we do? We touched it. Or at least some of us did.

As humans, we need to experience something before we change. Can we fix humans? Can we change this behavior? In short, no, we can't.

For example, when we send emails to our employees to verify if they'll click on potentially dangerous links once a year, we're not going to get the results we want. We're going to have people click the link. Instead of sending a yearly email to complete the audit, we need something more.

So let's be clear. If you experience it, you will listen and change.

Why We Need DevSecOps

Now let's look at the adversary's perspective. They have a large toolbox and a lot of time to do what they do.

On the organization's side, we have fewer tools and technologies. We also have policies, resources, and controls. They're not an effective tool against the adversary.

In short, we need help. We're erratic, conflicted, and disorganized. And we debate every decision. This is why we need DevSecOps.

Does that mean we need to spend more money on security? No. Currently we spend more than $124 billion in 2019. We're spending enough, but not in the right way. We're still expecting to hit $6 trillion in losses from security issues.

If Money Isn't the Answer, What Is?

So what do we need instead of more money?

▶ Communication

▶ Cooperation

▶ Coordination

▶ Collaboration

It's simple stuff. We don't need more tools from vendors. We need to focus on how we work with teams — security teams, design teams, development teams.

So how do we communicate in a way that others understand? It may not be a way that we're comfortable with. We might need to use terms that the business can understand. Networks are roads, IP addresses are mailboxes. Make it understandable.

And if we get it wrong, people can die. When we program autonomous vehicles, we need to account for things like jaywalking. Otherwise we'll end up with disastrous results.

Basics to Focus On

So what basics should we focus on?

First, fix the human — sort of. Even though we can't completely fix the human, we can make people understand that safety is not security. We should also remove the easy ways into our systems, and we should realize we don't have a perimeter. And once again, note that passwords are important.

All of these need a plan. So the final step is to get a plan.

One-hundred-percent security is a fallacy. We can only communicate our level of risk and reduce our level of risk.

Holding the Industry Accountable

The first way we hold our industry accountable is to look at our maturity model. What decisions and technology move the needle and reduce risk? Then let's talk about risk. Look at the business risk strategy and see how it compares to our risk strategy. And finally, measure it. If you have technology that's supposed to help, prove it.

DATA SECURITY MATURITY MODEL						
Security Maturity Levels >	0: Nonexistent	1: Initial	2: Repeatable	3: Defined	4: Managed	5: Optimized
Maturity Level Description >	There is no evidence of this standard or practice in the organization.	The organization has an ad hoc and inconsistent approach to this privacy standard or practice.	The organization has a consistent overall approach, but it is mostly undocumented.	The organization has a documented, detailed approach, but no routine measurement or enforcement of it.	The organization regularly measures its compliance and makes regular process improvements.	The organization has refined its compliance to the level of best practice.
process consistency	none	ad hoc	consistent	consistent	consistent	consistent
process documentation	none	none	minimal, high-level	detailed	detailed	detailed
business objectives	not met	not met	partially met	mostly met	fully met	value added
process measurement	none	none	none	ad hoc	routine	systemic
policy enforcement	none	none	none	ad hoc	routine	systemic
process improvement	none	ad hoc	ad hoc	ad hoc	routine	systemic
process benchmarking	none	none	none	ad hoc	ad hoc	routine
Corresponding Level of Risk of a Data Breach or Regulatory Noncompliance	Very high across the organization	High across the organization, and very high in key parts of the organization	Moderate across the organization, with some pockets of high risk	Moderate across the organization.	Low across the organization.	Remote across the organization.

Scorecard for Roberts's Data Security Maturity Model spreadsheet.

Using Roberts' reference material, you can then measure:

1. Where you are now

2. Where you want to be

3. Where you need to be

4. Where you have to be

If it seems overwhelming, don't worry. It shouldn't take more than two hours to complete. If it takes more than that, you're doing it wrong.

Areas to Focus

Think about detection and deception: we should always assume a breach. Then, if we assume breach, how will we know about it, and what are we going to do about it?

Until this point, we've approached technology in a reactive way. So how do we things differently? How do we engage someone earlier in the process? And how do we teach others earlier?

It's simple. We take an asymmetric shift to the blue team. We need to look at how we give the blue team more teeth.

On a final note, let's look at a fundamental attribution error. We play the blame game. Unless we know who was on the keyboard — what their motivations are — we can't do that. We need to look at ourselves in the mirror to see what we can do better.

Instead of focusing on blame, look to fix the problem.

We're all in this together. We need to sit down and work together. We need to collaborate because this is important. ∎

ABOUT THE PRESENTER

Chris Roberts will work with customers globally to develop and implement risk reduction strategies across new and legacy technologies. He will manage an advanced consulting services program which will provide compliance/assurance reviews to assess whether cybersecurity policies and standards are being met and to provide cybersecurity strategy and operations guidance for C-level executives. He will also be a key driver of strategy and vision around the Attivo Networks deception portfolio in areas where he has deep expertise including adversary and vulnerability research and market education. You can find Chris on Twitter at @Sidragon1.

Summary provided by Sylvia Fronczak.

Go to bit.ly/2020addo-roberts to watch the entire presentation.

Swim Don't Sink
Why Training Matters to an SRE Practice

presented by Jennifer Petoff

CHAPTER 22

Swim Don't Sink
Why Training Matters to an SRE Practice

I n this chapter, we're going to talk about why training matters and why the learning method of "sink or swim" doesn't cut it when you're ramping engineers up on your team.

Why Is Training Important?

With SRE, there's so much to learn. Many people believe that unleashing a firehose of information is an effective approach. However, we retain only a small percentage of the material presented to us in a lecture format. Because of this, the most important element of training is building confidence and fighting imposter syndrome. Training can also give your organizational culture a lift.

There are a variety of training options available on a continuum of effort:

1. Sink or swim

2. Self-study curriculum

3. Buddy system

4. Ad hoc classes

5. Systematic training programs

First, note that avoiding a "sink or swim" approach is important if you value inclusivity. "Sink or swim" breeds stress, frustration, attrition, and imposter syndrome.

Higher touch options signal leadership commitment to development, help ensure that everyone is speaking with one voice, and can reinforce desired behaviors to support a shift in organizational culture.

So what should you actually teach people?

The answer to this question is based on a few different factors:

▶ Maturity

▶ Familiarity

▶ Experience

Maturity refers to how far along on the SRE journey your organization is. *Familiarity* covers how familiar the individual is with your organization (are they new or have they worked here a long time?). *Experience* covers their background in SRE.

How to Build a Training Program for a Less Experienced Team

Here are some basic steps to get started if you are just starting out on your SRE journey as an organization.

Step 1: Address any skill gaps. Does your team have any common tools, defect tracking systems, or other necessary processes and knowledge?

Step 2: Know your team and tailor the message. For example, with people that have been in the organization for a long time, they may be resistant to adopting SRE principles, practices, and culture. They may think, "What's in it for me?" On the other hand, people new to the organization are more likely to go with the flow. If you have members of your team who have practiced SRE elsewhere, these are your catalysts. Let them share their stories.

Tailor your message for the people that make up your organization.

How to Build a Training Program for a High Maturity Case

What about organizations that already have an established SRE practice?

In this case, Step 1 involves assessing the team mix. Here, we have newbies, internal transfers, "old-timers," and industry veterans. Once you assess this mix, you'll want to take a look at what they all need.

Newbies, for example, need to learn your infrastructure, systems, and ways of working, while internal transfers likely need to focus more on learning SRE principles and practices rather than your specific systems.

Now let's consider what we add into our training program. You should look at both the what and the how. The *what* (training content) will be influenced by your mix of people, as we talked about above.

When looking at the *how*, consider how much effort you want to invest. The level of investment depends on (a) the size of your organization (b) how fast are you growing? For a small company, start with shadowing and mentoring. As the size of your organization increases, look at ongoing education options. Larger companies will get more benefit from investing in a structured training program.

What Can We Learn from SRE Principles and Apply to Training Operations?

Let's get meta for a moment and talk about how SRE principles can be applied to *running the training program itself*. Consider the service reliability hierarchy, a framework highlighted in the original SRE Book that covers the elements that go into making a service reliable, from most foundational to most advanced. We can then develop a training hierarchy in order to apply key SRE principles to training program operations.

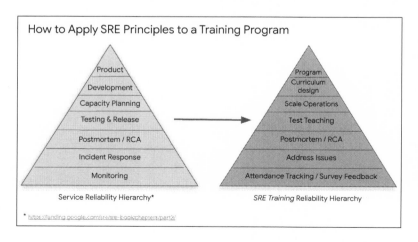

How to Apply SRE Principles to a Training Program

Service Reliability Hierarchy*

SRE Training Reliability Hierarchy

* https://landing.google.com/sre/sre-book/chapters/part3/

When developing your training, is more effort always better? No.

As with SRE practices, you should do just enough to meet the needs of your students. Keep them happy — but not too happy — and consider what tradeoffs you're making when creating your training program.

You should also monitor your trainings. Get feedback from your students and iterate.

For example, Google took feedback from their students that indicated training was passive and less engaging than they would have liked. So the team moved away from a lecture and made the training much more hands-on. They developed a training program that allowed the students to troubleshoot a problem. This provided them with immediate observable feedback on the effectiveness of the training. The monitoring reflected these improvements as well!

Key Takeaways

To sum it up, let's look at some key takeaways.

▶ **Training is an investment** — an investment in your organization and people.

▶ **Evaluate the cost and benefits** — to make sure you make the right level of investment.

▶ **Decide where to invest** — this depends on the what and how of your organizational circumstances.

▶ **Walk the Talk** — apply SRE / DevOps principles to the training program itself for a consistent and reliable experience.

Want to learn more? Read *Training Site Reliability Engineers: What Your Organization Needs to Create a Learning Program* ∎

ABOUT THE PRESENTER

Jennifer Petoff is a Senior Program Manager for Google's Site Reliability Engineering team based in Dublin, Ireland. She is the global lead for Google's SRE EDU program and is one of the co-editors of the best-selling book, *Site Reliability Engineering: How Google Runs Production Systems*.

Summary provided by Sylvia Fronczak.

Go to bit.ly/2020addo-petoff *to watch the entire presentation.*

Getting to Know the Entire Cybersecurity Industry for DevOps

presented by Richard Stiennon

CHAPTER 23

Getting to Know the Entire Cybersecurity Industry for DevOps

This story begins in 1993, when I was an automotive engineer in Detroit. I moved into the world of ISPs as the internet gained household popularity. Things really changed when I joined an MMSP that joined forces with Check Point software — a company that was foundational to what was to become the IT security industry. This company, started by Gil Shwed, Marius Nacht, and Shlomo Kramer, created the market for commercial firewalls. They ended up largely responsible for the tech investment culture in Israel.

It wasn't a straight path to success. Instead, it is a winding tale of opportunities and connections that contributed to the way that security is marketed today.

Is the Security Industry Consolidating?

One thing you may hear today is that the security industry is consolidating. Stiennon tells us that consolidation is a myth.

First, it's not consolidation when, say, a company like McAfee acquires additional security companies. This is a larger company looking for opportunities and acquiring companies that show potential. More and more companies enter the space every year, finding unique niches in the security space.

Another myth around cybersecurity involves growth. In fact, growth is misstated:

You can't grow from $2.5B in 2003 to $85B in 2013 at 9% CAGR (compound annual growth rate). It's more like 34% CAGR. If the industry is really growing that fast, then perhaps we really don't understand the size of the industry.

An Increase in Security Interest

Early on, threat actors weren't as organized as they are today. That changed in 2003, thanks to the KGB and other actors, when cybercrime really took off. Additionally, cyber espionage kicked off a few years later. By 2013, Edward Snowden famously exposed the depth of NSA surveillance.

As these efforts grew, IT security spending grew as well. Now we're at a point where we're spending $335B on security. This won't slow down until the threat actors go home or slow down.

Answer: No, We're Not Consolidating

So let's take a look again at the companies involved in all this spending. First, it's interesting to note that of all the companies involved in security, few exist in the cloud security category. Additionally, back to the point about consolidation, if we have 2,336+ companies, then we don't have consolidation.

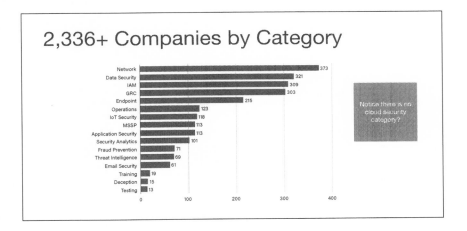

The categories of companies cover a large variety of security needs. Early in the timeline, we started with network, data security, IAM, GRC (governance, risk, and compliance), and endpoint security vendors.

Now we've got a lot of new buckets that show the lack of consolidation again.

Ending With a Discussion of Categories of Growth

There's plenty of evidence for growth in the cybersecurity industry. For example, there's the security operation centers where we see people sitting in rooms monitoring security across large screens. This group will soon be automating responses to threats as they start to occur.

Another area of growth includes IOT security: not only for the IOT devices in your home but also in manufacturing and wherever devices exist.

Then there is application security. Application security is most familiar to us. That entails writing secure code and automating checks to verify that the developers deploy secure code.

Security analytics is growing as well. That's because we have too much data. We're not just finding the needle in the haystack but the needle in the needlestack. We need to analyze data to know when we're getting attacked and to know how to stop the attack.

There's also fraud prevention, which includes identity verification. It can work to prevent fraud in your organization and make sure that sales are valid. These companies also get bought up by Visa and other players in the credit market.

Other categories exist and new ones emerge frequently. Overall, the entire security industry is a growing and expanding field. New opportunities will continue to develop as the industry matures and threat actors find new vulnerabilities and opportunities. It is growing, not slowing. ∎

ABOUT THE PRESENTER

Richard Stiennon is Chief Research Analyst for IT-Harvest, the firm he founded in 2005 to cover the 2,337 vendors that make up the IT security industry. He has presented on the topic of cybersecurity in 31 countries on six continents. He was a lecturer at Charles Sturt University in Australia. He is the author of *Surviving Cyberwar* (Government Institutes, 2010) and Washington Post Best Seller, There Will Be Cyberwar. He writes for *Forbes*, *CSO Magazine*, and *The Analyst Syndicate*. He is a member of the advisory board at the Information Governance Initiative. Stiennon was Chief Strategy Officer for Blancco Technology Group, the Chief Marketing Officer for Fortinet, Inc. and VP Threat Research at Webroot Software. Prior to that he was VP Research at Gartner, Inc. He has a B.S. in Aerospace Engineering and his MA in War in the Modern World from King's College, London. His latest book *Security Yearbook 2020* is available on Amazon.

Summary provided by Sylvia Fronczak.

Go to bit.ly/2020addo-stiennon *to watch the entire presentation.*

OWASP Security Knowledge Framework

presented by Glenn ten Cate and Riccardo ten Cate

CHAPTER 24

OWASP Security Knowledge Framework

D evOps is more achievable than ever, with plenty of available materials on what it is and how to get started with it. But how should you incorporate security into it? This is the challenge of DevSecOps.

Secure Software Development Life Cycle (SSDLC)

The secure software development life cycle is a method to help web and app developers establish best practices at each stage of product development. What are the parts of this method, and why does it make sense to use it?

COMPONENTS

An SSDLC relies on four parts:

1. Security requirements

2. Test automation and code quality checks

3. Security test automation

4. Manual verification

Let's talk about each of these in turn.

Security Requirements

It's critical that you gather security requirements before starting work. Otherwise, you'll miss requirements and struggle to secure your application at the end.

Test Automation and Code Quality Checks

Dead end code, overly complex code, and repudiated code each present potential vulnerabilities. Automation makes finding these easier than doing so by hand.

Security Test Automation

Security test automation is common in DevOps processes and comes in two flavors: static analyzers (SAST) look at source code, and dynamic analyzers (DAST) inspect a running application. That said, they detect only about 20% of the 280 controls in the OWASP application security verification system.

In addition, these analyzers present two more challenges beyond struggling to find vulnerabilities. First, you must verify all findings manually. Second, running the analyzers requires architecture considerations such as containers to run the applications, plus tests and tools to track and manage the findings.

Manual Verification

Because all analyzer findings need manual verification, false positives are a nightmare for security engineers. You'll want to track false positives across builds, and that requires additional tools.

BETTER AUTOMATED SECURITY TOOLING

Automated security tooling has a place in the SSDLC, but we need something more effective: developers. Developers are the most effective tool for building apps that are secure by design. Developers make a lot of the same coding mistakes over and over, and as a result, some developers are barely hanging on. Instead, developers should be in control and confidently build secure apps.

Fortunately, there's a way to do this: the Security Knowledge Framework, developed five years ago by Glenn, Riccardo, and several other contributors.

Security Knowledge Framework

The security knowledge framework (SKF), part of OWASP, helps you write more secure apps by:

▶ Guiding you to a secure application design instead of thinking about security after the fact

▶ Informing you about threats before a single line of source code is written

▶ Providing information that applies to your needs on the spot

▶ Setting up the right security requirements for your project

The SKF relies heavily on OWASP's application security verification standard (ASVS) and its security controls. The ASVS has 4 levels: Cursory (level 0); Opportunistic (level 1); Standard (level 2); and Advanced (level 3). With this in mind, start at level 1 unless your industry or situation dictates starting elsewhere. For example, banks should be at level 3 and use all the controls.

Code analyzers find injection and configuration vulnerabilities pretty well, but they miss issues in application logic. In contrast, the SKF gives developers both the right security requirements and the right mindset for success.

SKF IN DEPTH

The security knowledge framework website has a live demo you can check out. From there, you can install and host the SKF app internally for your own use. The SKF website has a chatbot that will link you to OWASP resources based on questions you enter. The SKF has four main sections:

▶ Labs

▶ Checklists

▶ Knowledge base

▶ Projects

Labs

Labs in the SKF provide a live example of each issue through containerized code.

Checklists

Checklists break the ASVS into categories for easier consumption. To start, use a checklist to help assess your project against the ASVS, as all the controls are linked to knowledge base articles.

Knowledge Base

Every ASVS control has a knowledge base article describing the attack vector and solution with accompanying code samples.

Projects

A project in SKF links work on your team to your security requirements through checklists and ASVS controls. Also, you can lay out your security requirements in sprints to break them down for tracking purposes.

Conclusion

The goal of this talk was to move developers from barely hanging on, security-wise, to confidently building apps that are secure by design. As shown above, the SKF fuels that transition.

Use the SKF to gather security requirements, schedule them for implementation, and track their assessment. When you do, you'll unlock the power of developers as security champions through OWASP and SKF. ∎

ABOUT THE PRESENTERS

As a coder, hacker, speaker, trainer and security researcher employed at ING bank in Belgium as the Security Manager, **Glenn ten Cate** has over 15 years experience in the field of security. He is one of the founders of defensive development def[dev]eu — a security training series dedicated to helping you build and maintain secure software and has also spoken at multiple other security conferences in the world. His goal is to create an open-source software development life cycle with the tools and knowledge gathered over the years.

As a penetration tester from the Netherlands, **Riccardo ten Cate** specializes in application security and has extensive knowledge in securing applications in multiple coding languages. He has many years of experience in training and guiding development teams becoming more mature and making their applications secure by design. Riccardo also has expertise on implementing security test automation in CI/CD pipelines. This helps create short feedback loops back to the developer and prevents bugs from getting into production into an early phase of the development lifecycle.

Summary provided by Daniel Longest.

Go to bit.ly/2020addo-tencate to watch the entire presentation.

CHAPTER 25

Can Kubernetes Keep a Secret?

presented by Omer Levi Hevroni

CHAPTER 25

Can Kubernetes Keep a Secret?

E very application uses secrets to function. These secrets include usernames and passwords, API keys, and other similar private keys. Applications running inside Kubernetes are no exception. Unfortunately, Kubernetes has a reputation for not being able to keep a secret. Is that reputation valid?

Who Handles Secrets?

A centralized management team oversees secrets in some companies as part of running deployments. The alternative model, though, is Super Devs with full responsibility for writing code, deploying it, and monitoring it. On the one hand, a centralized team manages secrets securely. On the other hand, Super Devs yield a simpler and more scalable organization. That said, Super Devs need good tools to support them, to minimize mistakes, and to make systems secure by design.

GitOps

Developers are already familiar with Git. As a result, there are many upsides to relying on Git for the entire workflow, referred to as GitOps. Typically, code and Kubernetes manifest files live in the repository. Then, they are deployed from there into Kubernetes pods. However, what about the application secrets that must be stored securely?

Requirements

The goal was to find a solution that met these requirements:

► Embraces GitOps

► Integrates natively with Kubernetes

► Stores secrets securely by design

For this analysis, security related to the Kubernetes pod is out of scope. For example, SSH access to the pod and secret leakage from the pod are interesting subjects but not part of this analysis.

Options

OPTION 1: KUBERNETES SECRETS

Kubernetes Secrets are the official Kubernetes means of storing secrets securely. They're intended for use on SSH keys, OAuth tokens, and passwords. By comparison, Kubernetes Secrets are safer and more flexible than deploying directly in the pod or a docker image.

Here's the issue though. Kubernetes Secrets store usernames and passwords as base-64 encoded strings. As a result, they're obscured from casual browsing, but this is still the same as being in plaintext. To emphasize, text encoding isn't secure. As a result, Kubernetes Secrets as a solution are immediately complicated.

Encrypting Secrets

What about encrypting secrets? Sealed secrets and Helm secrets are two options. Sealed secrets result in encrypted secrets in the manifest file that are decrypted in the pod. On the one hand, that seems to do the trick. However, there are still issues. First, for sealed secrets, anyone with access to the cluster can decrypt the secrets. Second, you're coupled to the specific cluster and deployment method for Helm secrets. Lastly, any changes to the encrypted secrets require decryption, and this affects other configurations within the same file.

Evaluation

Compared to the requirements, this solution integrates natively with Kubernetes, but both the GitOps and "secure by design" requirements are only met with serious limitations.

OPTION 2: HASHICORP'S VAULT

The next option relies on HashiCorp's Vault system to store secrets securely. Vault lives side by side with the applications. First, developers put app secrets into Vault. Then, the applications contact Vault to receive plaintext secrets as needed. The workflow sounds simple but has an issue: access control.

Fairly significant permissions issues exist on Vault as compared to the requirements. First, some developers need access to manage secrets, while others only need read access. Consequently, you'll still require a centralized management team. In addition, Vault receives secrets directly, rather than from Git, so GitOps isn't supported. Lastly, central management of secrets in Vault has advantages but one big disadvantage. Specifically, there's no single source of truth for application configuration inclusive of code, Kubernetes manifest, and secrets. As a result, troubleshooting is more difficult.

Evaluation

Compared to the requirements, this solution integrates natively with Kubernetes but doesn't use GitOps. Also the "secure by design" requirement depends on specific usage.

OPTION 3: KAMUS

Both mainstream solutions didn't meet the needs for protecting secrets in Kubernetes. In time, inspiration came from Travis CI. Specifically, Travis supports a command-line function to encrypt parameters. In similar fashion, could Kubernetes support such a function? With this in mind, Kamus was born.

Kamus encrypts secrets for a specific application. Subsequently, only that application receives the plaintext. As a result, even if other pods try to decrypt the secret, they'll fail. First, Kamus encrypts the secret to go into the Git repository using the intended application's service account token. Then, the pod sends the encrypted secret and its Kubernetes service account to Kamus to receive plaintext secrets. In effect, the service account provides the assurance for Kamus to decrypt secrets for the application.

Additional Details

Kamus leverages cloud encryption services like Azure Key Vault, thus hardware security modules (HSMs) are supported. Also, Kamus supports cloud resource definitions (CRDs) for Kubernetes Secrets.

The permission model for Kamus is straightforward. First, users can encrypt on a limited basis but cannot decrypt. Next, a pod can encrypt but can only decrypt its own secrets.

Evaluation

Compared to the requirements, this solution meets them all: full GitOps support, native Kubernetes integration, and secure secrets by design.

Wrapping Up

Can Kubernetes keep a secret? Based on this talk, yes. To be sure, you need the right tool for your business. To that end, Kamus enables your Super Devs to fly higher. ∎

ABOUT THE PRESENTER

Omer Levi Hevroni has been writing code for the last 10 years and working at Soluto for the last 3 years as Software Developer and Security Champion.

Summary provided by Daniel Longest.

Go to bit.ly/2020addo-hevroni to watch the entire presentation.

Building Secure & Reliable Systems

A Conversation With the Authors of Google's SRE Book

*presented by Betsy Beyer, Paul Blankinship,
Piotr Lewandowski, and Dave Rensin*

CHAPTER 26

Building Secure & Reliable Systems
A Conversation With the Authors
of Google's SRE Book

I n this interview, Dave Rensin talks with book editors Betsy Beyer, Paul Blankinship, and Piotr Lewandowski about the Google SRE book from O'Reilly: *Building Secure & Reliable Systems: Best Practices for Designing, Implementing, and Maintaining Systems.*

Why This Book Matters

Dave Rensin: What was the need for this latest book?

Betsy Beyer: As a lot of you know, we've put out two other SRE-focused books, and we knew there was an appetite for more information on SRE and on how Google implements security. People want to know how security and reliability go together. Based on what we've learned, security and reliability go hand in hand to create the building blocks of a reliable system.

Why Security and Reliability Together?

Dave Rensin: What is so special about security and reliability that made you want to write a book about it? There are other books on security, and there are other books on reliability. What was the impetus to pair them together in this case?

Piotr Lewandowski: I've been watching this space for the better part of a decade. Usually, areas that fall between organizational boundaries get overlooked and don't get enough attention. Those weakest spots reveal themselves, which presents opportunities to improve security.

One of the main things the authors want to share is that you need both security and reliability and you can't have one without the other. Everyone is responsible for both but SREs often see themselves as the last line of defense for both security and reliability. Why is that? They need to keep up to date with infrastructure changes and because of that, components that passed security audits two years ago might not pass one today. SREs are in the best position to identify those gaps.

Why So Many Animals in the Zoo?

Dave Rensin: There are more than 100 authors in this book. Why so many people? Why so many animals in the zoo?

Paul Blankinship: At Google, we have a lot of good people, and it's easy to ask people to contribute to these topics. We're looking at things from a design perspective. So, in order to bring in the best people for each chapter, we brought in the people that we thought could speak the most comprehensively to each topic.

Main Takeaways for Readers

Dave Rensin: Pick a small number of things you want readers to take away when they read the book.

Betsy Beyer: The basic premise is that we really want people to start shifting their approach to security and reliability to the left. Both need to be considered as early as possible in the life cycle. Because if you tack them on at the end, it won't be as effective. It will also be more expensive.

Piotr Lewandowski: In addition to shifting security and reliability left, people need to think about the organization, and they need to think about how to implement reliability and security into the organization. You need to see the organization as a system to understand how to integrate security and reliability, and make sure your culture reflects that the work is everyone's responsibility in order to protect your customers and the data they have trusted you with.

Paul Blankinship: It's sometimes hard for small startups to spend money on security and reliability. In part, this is because you can't always clearly see the benefits of improved security. You can't demonstrate what didn't happen, or wouldn't have happened without the security you put into place. There are lots of arguments in this book for adding in security early. The book shows that security and reliability are important to the architecture of systems, and not easily added once your system is built out.

Dave Rensin: There's a point a lot of people misunderstand. There's a holy trinity that you need to consider: scalability, reliability, and multi-tenancy.

Are There Things You Wished They'd Included But Didn't?

Dave Rensin: What do you wish you would have been able to add to the book?

Betsy Beyer: There were a lot of case studies that we wanted to add, but we couldn't publish a 1,200-page book. As is the case with the last couple of books, we still have extra content. We'll find ways to publish that content. It's not the last you've heard from Google on these topics.

Paul Blankinship: We wanted this book to be helpful for all sizes of companies. There were a lot of stories that we could tell that were specific to Google, but that might not be generally helpful. So despite the fact that these stories and anecdotes were interesting, these stories didn't make it.

Betsy Beyer: We should have added an addendum of interesting but useless anecdotes?

Piotr Lewandowski: The problem was that we wanted to create a book that applied to a broad range of companies — from startups to large companies. So we had to axe a few pieces that didn't apply to small companies.

"Well, I Heard at Google That..."

Dave Rensin: Everyone's mentioned it to one degree or another: Whenever I talk to people about reliability, and particularly about Google SRE, two times out of 10, three times out of 10, someone starts the question with "Well, I heard at Google that...," and it's something weird like "I heard you sacrifice small animals for the safety of your data center" or something like that. I'm curious: Are there misconceptions of the way you do security or reliability at scale at Google that you want to address head-on here?

Paul Blankinship: Looking at Google from the outside, it seems like a big monolithic company with lots of very smart people doing very smart things. In reality Google employees are people, just like the employees of other companies. People make mistakes. The information in the book isn't valuable because we have the brightest people in the world, but because we've tried a lot of things. One thing that's really impressive about Google is the culture of blameless postmortems. It's a great way to learn and grow from mistakes.

Dave Rensin: We do things wrong to figure out how to do things right.

Piotr Lewandowski: One misconception is that some people may think that we write about blameless postmortems but don't really follow that rule. But we really do follow it. Sometimes there's a culture mismatch when people join from different backgrounds. We introduce the concept of blameless postmortems as one of the first things. We want to learn from our mistakes in a constructive and sustainable way and therefore we write a lot of postmortems, even for smaller, internal incidents and not just the large things that hit the press.

Dave Rensin: Our finance team even writes postmortems, looking at what went well and what could be improved. They use the SRE postmortem template and even file bugs!

Betsy Beyer: Google is not a monolith. Not all teams approach reliability in the same way. Tools and methodologies vary between systems and teams. There are a lot of different effective ways to accomplish reliability goals.

Dave Rensin: Many organizations have separate dev and separate security groups.

Conclusion

A lot of work and decades of experience in security and reliability went into this book. A wealth of knowledge from industry experts can be found in just a single chapter. For recommendations from each panelist on which chapter they suggest you read, watch the panel. ∎

ABOUT THE PRESENTERS

Betsy Beyer is a NYC-based staff technical writer at Google who specializes in Site Reliability Engineering. She co-edited *Site Reliability Engineering: How Google Runs Production Systems* and *The Site Reliability Workbook*. En route to her current career, Betsy studied International Relations and English Literature, and holds degrees from Stanford and Tulane.

Dave Rensin is a Senior Director of Engineering in the Office of the CFO, where he serves on a small team of technical advisers to Alphabet's CFO. Dave provides guidance on the appropriate allocation of Google's capital to its various businesses and long-term technical investments. Prior to that, Dave founded Customer Reliability Engineering (CRE) and also ran Google's global network capacity planning. He has more than 25 years experience designing and delivering planet-scale cloud and mobile products. Prior to joining Google, Dave worked at Amazon on their classified (now declassified) C2S project. As an entrepreneur, he has co-founded and sold several businesses including one (Riverbed Technologies) for more than $1 billion,and has served as an officer in two publicly traded companies (Omnisky and Aether). He is also a bestselling author and editor with 16 US patents to his name. Dave earned a degree in Statistics from the University of Maryland, and is married with three children.

Piotr Lewandowski is a Senior Staff Site Reliability Engineer, and has spent the past nine years improving the security posture of Google's infrastructure. As the Production Tech Lead for Security, he is responsible for harmonious collaboration between the SRE and security organizations. In his previous role, he led a team responsible for the reliability of Google's critical security infrastructure. Before joining Google, he built a startup, worked at CERT Polska, and got a degree in computer science from Warsaw University of Technology.

Paul Blankinship manages the Technical Writing team for Google's Security and Privacy Engineering group, and has helped develop Google's internal security and privacy policies. In addition to his career as a technical writer, he is a performing musician in the SF Bay Area.

Summary provided by Sylvia Fronczak.

Go to bit.ly/2020addo-beyer *to watch the entire presentation.*

You've Convinced Me We Have to Collaborate

But How The Hell Do We Deal With People?

presented by Matt Stratton

CHAPTER 27

You've Convinced Me We Have to Collaborate

But How The Hell Do We Deal With People?

We hear "collaboration" and "breaking down silos" a lot with DevOps. We often follow it up with terms like "empathy," but how do we actually apply empathy? By understanding that collaboration is central to effective DevOps teams.

DORA Leads the Way

One leader in figuring out how to effectively apply empathy when collaborating is DORA and the *2019 State of the DevOps* report. They pursued how organizations like Google became high performing. Do they have some special sauce? Or are there strategies and practices we can repeat at other organizations? It turns out that Google has a lot of psychological safety, and this is key for ensuring strong collaboration.

Psychological Safety

Although it is a key factor in Google's success, the term "psychological safety" can be vague. Other companies that wish to model psychological safety in their organization may be unsure of what it entails.

The definition we are going by is this: Psychological safety is a sense of confidence that the team will not punish or embarrass someone for speaking up.

Now, many teams believe they have this. They may say things like "We are all nice around each other." But that doesn't necessarily mean the team is psychologically safe. For example, Matt made a sarcastic comment to a longtime friend on his team in a work chat room. While his friend understood it was a joke, that sharp comment signaled to people outside the team that this was potentially a psychologically unsafe team.

Psychological safety is a sense of confidence that the team will not punish or embarrass someone for speaking up.

Amy Edmondson, Professor at Harvard Business School

Conflict

While we want to avoid making people feel that a team is psychologically unsafe, we also don't want to avoid conflict. Conflict is necessary for collaboration, but we have to approach it correctly. Sometimes it's necessary to step back and remind yourself that your teammates want to accomplish the same goal as you do, even though you may differ on the approach.

We want to talk through disagreements as one human to another.

Although we all have differences, as humans, we are more alike than different. Thinking about this during our discourse is a powerful tool to foster empathy.

Blamelessness, Curiosity, and Vulnerability

We also want to replace blame with curiosity. Humans are imperfect, and none of us has all the facts or perfect objectivity. So, if we come in with a curious mindset of "what do I not yet know," instead of "how do I prove that I'm right," we create psychological safety.

Sometimes curiosity comes off as vulnerability, and this is actually a good thing. People may think that being vulnerable is exposing weakness. But really it's showing our humanity. People will be more willing to bring forth their ideas when they know it's OK to not be perfect.

Even though we want curiosity, we are still hardwired to lay blame.

This means we need to facilitate conversations to actively steer away from blame. Here are some tips:

▶ Encourage people to speak up to ensure that everyone is heard.

▶ Clarify insights and challenge your team with questions. Questions, especially open-ended ones, often express curiosity.

▶ Don't make decisions or take sides as a facilitator. Your job is to guide the conversation, not to solve the problem.

▶ Try to speak as little as possible. Your job is to let others speak as equally as possible.

De-Escalating Conflict

Despite all our efforts to create a psychologically safe culture, potentially unhealthy conflicts sometimes arise, and we need to bring the conflict to a stop to reset.

This is not about compromising but about letting everyone feel heard. When people feel heard, they will often de-escalate their emotions. The factors to de-escalate, in order, are:

▶ **Observations.** Before making judgments, we must observe what each person is doing and saying. We also should understand what they are observing.

▶ **Feelings.** From observation, we can extract how people are feeling. An angry arguer is different from a sad arguer.

▶ **Needs.** What does each person in the room need from the conversation? People who have strong feelings are often not getting what they need.

▶ **Requests.** These are the concrete actions that people would like to be taken. Ask questions like "Would you be willing to...?" This will help people get on the same page.

Conclusion

We know collaboration with empathy is important, but we may not know how to achieve it. We must understand that it is important to create psychological safety in a team where everyone can speak with confidence and without fear of embarrassment. We can do this through blameless curiosity and facilitating conversations that de-escalate conflict. We are wired for blame, and we must actively steer discussions away from it. ∎.

ABOUT THE PRESENTER

Matt Stratton is a Transformation Specialist at Red Hat and a long-time member of the global DevOps community. Back in the day, his license plate actually said "DevOps."

Matt has over 20 years of experience in IT operations, ranging from large financial institutions such as JPMorganChase to internet firms including Apartments.com. He is a sought-after speaker internationally, presenting at Agile, DevOps, and ITSM focused events, including DevOps Enterprise Summit, DevOpsDays, Interop, PINK, and others worldwide. Matt is the founder and co-host of the popular Arrested DevOps podcast, as well as a global organizer of the DevOpsDays set of conferences.

He lives in Chicago and has three awesome kids — Henry, Joey, and Sophia, who he loves just a little bit more than he loves "Doctor Who." He is currently on a mission to discover the best pho in the world.

Summary provided by Mark Henke

Go to bit.ly/2020addo-stratton *to watch the entire presentation.*

How to Be a Strong Leader in Disruptive Times

presented by Charlene Li

CHAPTER 28

How to Be a Strong Leader in Disruptive Times

Taming chaos and handling disruption takes courage. Disruption comes when we don't feel in control, when we're unsure about the future, and when stability is shaken. However, we can see disruption as an opportunity to lead change.

5 Ways Leadership Must Change

In order to deal with disruption effectively, leadership must change. Here are five ways to lead through disruptive times:

1. Embrace a disruption mindset.
2. Use structure to establish stability and security.
3. Be open and transparent to keep everyone on the same page and establish credibility.
4. Communicate a strong vision for the future that others can almost taste.
5. Find opportunities for the future. This may take innovation, creativity, and inspiration.

Recognize Your Leadership Style

There are many types, archetypes, and styles of leadership. Each style of leadership has its place in the world, especially when disruption is involved. What is your leadership archetype? Are you a steadfast manager who might not be so open to change but loves to inspire others? How about a worried skeptic who doesn't like change and prefers to

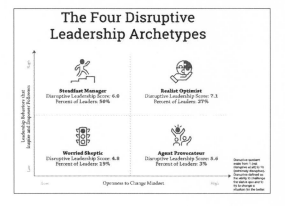

The Four Disruptive Leadership Archetypes

Steadfast Manager
Disruptive Leadership Score: 6.8
Percent of Leaders: 50%

Realist Optimist
Disruptive Leadership Score: 7.1
Percent of Leaders: 27%

Worried Skeptic
Disruptive Leadership Score: 4.8
Percent of Leaders: 19%

Agent Provocateur
Disruptive Leadership Score: 5.6
Percent of Leaders: 3%

just keep a low profile? All leaders can change with the right mindset. Think about what the change means for the organization.

Everyone has a place during disruptive times. Organizations need leaders who think about what can go wrong just as much as they need those who can motivate everyone in the right direction. Effective managers of all archetypes need to work together and combine their strengths to reach the other side.

Create Stability

In order to create stability, try to use as many of the same tools and processes as possible during the disruption. The onset of disruption will cause instability and uncertainty. Rituals, processes, and tools might need to change, but some amount of familiarity will keep others from suffering from change fatigue.

For someone who is resistant to change, meaning they have a low disruption quotient, anything you, as a leader, can do to maintain the status quo during highly disruptive times is essential for their productivity and wellbeing.

Be Open

Openness creates a sense of accountability and increases diversity. Leaders who are open set the example for others to be open. When that happens, failure becomes an opportunity to learn rather something to fear. The diversity that openness creates allows everyone to bring ideas to the table, which is great for both the team and the organization!

How do you know what to be open about? Charlene recommends finding the areas where trust is low and being more open about those topics. Private information should still be private. Being open doesn't necessarily mean sharing salary information with everyone; it means giving everyone the information that enables them to make better decisions.

Communicate in 3D

The three dimensions of 3D communication are:

▶ Over communicating

▶ Being multi-modal

▶ Thinking remote-first

These three dimensions help to keep the vision solidified in the minds of others through repeated messaging over different modes of communication. Some people remember what they read better than others. Others may best internalize what they see or hear. So, when you communicate what's important, use words, images, and verbal reminders to make sure everyone receives the message well.

Remote thinking means setting up communications with the expectation that people are not in the same physical space. Posters, for example, can't reach remote workers. Also, meetings need to enable remote workers to access the same information as everyone in the room. This might mean cameras in the room to show body language, shared screens and documents, and technology that is capable of delivering everything on time, every time.

Disruption Leads to Innovation

Every recession led to major innovations such as the iPod, CNN, and Uber (and other gig culture companies). Leaders set the pace for innovation by being open and honest.

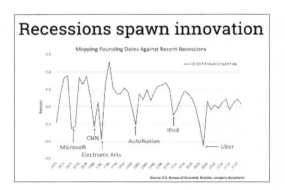

Lead the Future

It takes disruption to spur true innovation. World-changing events like major recessions and pandemics create vast opportunities for leaders to make the world a better place. Disruption doesn't have to cause companies to fail, but it does cause companies to change. ∎

ABOUT THE PRESENTER

For the past two decades, **Charlene Li** has been helping people see the future. She's an expert on digital transformation, leadership, customer experience and the future of work. She's the author of six books, including the New York Times bestseller, *Open Leadership* and co-author of the critically acclaimed book, *Groundswell*. Her latest book is the bestseller *The Disruption Mindset*. She is the Founder and Senior Fellow at Altimeter, an analyst firm acquired in 2015 by Prophet. Named one of the most creative people in business by *Fast Company*, Charlene is a graduate of Harvard College and Harvard Business School.

Summary provided by Phil Vuollet.

Go to bit.ly/2020addo-li *to watch the entire presentation.*

Continuous Verification and the Myths of Reliability

presented by Casey Rosenthal

CHAPTER 29

Continuous Verification and the Myths of Reliability

A leader put together a research project regarding the ships. He looked at how successful the ships' routes were, how risky the ships were to sail on, and the mortality rate of the ships.

To give you an idea of what life was like on these ships, it was fairly dangerous but profitable. There was a fortune to be made and an incentive to take risks. Though the captains had the same weather reports, the ship captains made different decisions based on their risk tolerance.

The captains that took more risks typically were more profitable. Interestingly, the captains that took more risks also had lower mortality. That's because they built up their skills to deal with surprises at sea. The ones that didn't take risks didn't know how to deal with surprises.

Shoes and Resilience

Back in the 1850s, the streets were filthy, and people constantly needed to get new shoes. So the shoe industry grew rapidly. The shoe stores had racers that would make marks with chalk to indicate how many shoes were needed at different locations. This worked when things were slow, but when things were hectic, people would get ahead of themselves and mark extra chalk marks, in anticipation for additional shoe needs. Then, the wrong number of shoes would show up.

Again, small decisions were causing larger outside impacts. People were making what they thought were the right decisions, but from a higher level, it caused issues.

Tying it Back to Software

The key is that we're trying to balance between economics, workload, and safety.

For example, you probably don't want engineers to spin up 1,000 instances of a service. There might not be a rule against this, but you expect engineers to understand that these instances cost money. This doesn't need to be explained because they understand the implications.

Similarly, engineers negotiate workload because they understand that there's a margin that they can't stretch. With safety, it's similar, but there's one difference. Security folks don't always know how far to stretch. We still have security incidents. In fact, we can't stop security incidents before they happen because we don't know about them until they happen.

Enter Chaos Engineering

So what can we do? We can build in chaos engineering. By adding chaos into the system, we can become more resilient to risk. Chaos engineering can help us move the needle on security and reliability.

The chief merit of [software engineering] is its technical efficiency, with a premium placed on precision, speed, expert control, continuity, discretion, and optimal returns on input.

Robert K. Merton

The quote above about software engineering shared by Rosenthal is actually about bureaucracy. But it applies to software engineering. After all, software engineering is a bureaucratic profession. Why? Because no one decides how the work needs to be done, or what work needs to be done, from the people that actually do the work.

We have team leads, managers, architects... all pull the decisions away from the software engineers that have been hired to solve the problems.

Many companies view this as the ideal model. This goes back to scientific management as it works for manufacturing widgets. But we're not manufacturing widgets. We're doing knowledge work. Here, you want the engineers to be empowered to solve the problems.

What Are the Myths of Reliability?

Let's look at some myths.

MYTH 1: REMOVING THE PEOPLE WHO CAUSE ACCIDENTS WILL SOLVE THE PROBLEM.

They tried to do this in a hospital by removing the doctors that had the most accidents. However, what they found is that those doctors knew how to deal with difficult situations. Malpractice suits went up because inexperienced people didn't know how to deal with those situations.

MYTH 2: DOCUMENT BEST PRACTICES AND RUNBOOKS.

Why doesn't this work? Now, we're not saying don't document things. However, the skills necessary for a resilient system requires improvisation. You can't always communicate an adaptive capacity through the written word. Usually, it doesn't work.

MYTH 3: DEFEND AGAINST PRIOR ROOT CAUSES.

The problem with this particular myth is that, in a complex system, there are no root causes. You can't blame someone for writing a bad algorithm. The developer was optimizing for the directions given. So it could be the manager's fault, or the VP's fault, or maybe even the CTO's fault for not setting context and alignment.

Additional risks can be found around enforcing procedures and avoiding risks. But guardrails don't help.

Takeaways

Again, we can't take all the complexity out of complex systems. We build resilience by being confronted with problems. Add chaos to your systems to build your system resiliency and your engineer's resiliency knowledge, and you'll be poised to succeed. ■

ABOUT THE PRESENTER

Casey Rosenthal is CEO and cofounder of Verica; formerly the Engineering Manager of the Chaos Engineering Team at Netflix. He has experience with distributed systems, artificial intelligence, translating novel algorithms and academia into working models, and selling a vision of the possible to clients and colleagues alike. His superpower is transforming misaligned teams into high performance teams, and his personal mission is to help people see that something different, something better, is possible. For fun, he models human behavior using personality profiles in Ruby, Erlang, Elixir, and Prolog.

Summary provided by Sylvia Fronczak.

Go to bit.ly/2020addo-rosenthal *to watch the entire presentation.*

Human or Machine?
The Voight-Kampff Test for Discovering Web Application Vulnerabilities

presented by Vanessa Sauter

CHAPTER 30

Human or Machine?
The Voight-Kampff Test for Discovering Web Application Vulnerabilities

How can we apply the Voight-Kampff test to detect web application vulnerabilities? This topic is important because there is not a ton of research on how to appropriately penetration test or ethically hack into their own applications. But even more so, discerning between human and machine is a way of discerning value in a results-driven market. Specialized pen testers are competing against open-source tool developers.

Hacker Report

The *2019 Hacker Report* shows for one bug bounty company, 90% of targets were web applications.

We will take these results to the next level and show what vulnerabilities humans can find versus what vulnerabilities machines can find.

But first, let's establish some basic terms and talk about what they mean.

A Quick Explainer

To go to the next level, we will talk about black-box penetration testing, as well as dynamic scanners.

Black-box penetration testing, or pen testing, is where we have no access to the source code and no internal knowledge. In this testing, you come in relatively blind, relying on your general knowledge and public access points to a software system.

In dynamic scanning, you are analyzing applications at runtime. With this, you have internal accounts and other tooling to access applications with internal knowledge.

There are also proxies, where hackers can intercept HTTP requests between an application and its users.

Findings

We can find out quite a lot with all these tools at our disposal. For starters, the number one cause of web application vulnerabilities is misconfigured application settings. This includes anything from insecure business logic to cookie settings.

We also found that machines are better at detecting the vast majority of vulnerabilities. For example, they can find cross-site scripting issues much faster than any human.

Much of the time, the machine wins because they are being "told" what to look for, especially with DAST/OAST testing:

The Machine Wins

- ✓ XXS (Self, Stored, and Reflected)
- ✓ SQL (Including Blind and Second-Order)
- ✓ SSRF
- ✓ CSRF
- ✓ Sensitive Information Disclosure
  - • Path Traversal
  - • Application Errors
  - • Directory Listing
- ✓ Missing or Broken Authentication

- ✓ Security Headers
  - • Clickjacking (UI Redressing)
- ✓ Components with Known Vulns
- ✓ Local and Remote File Inclusion
- ✓ Cookie Attributes
- ✓ SSL/TLS-Related Issues
- ✓ OS Command Injection
- ✓ XXE
- ✓ CORS-Related Issues

There's an argument that humans are better at knowing where to look. Therefore, they should instruct the machine to go find all instances of whatever it is that the human seeks.

There are a variety of tools that can do this work for us, but we have to calculate the cost of configuring these tools versus the time they save us in continually finding vulnerabilities.

Where the Human Wins

The human wins in a few situations. This includes business logic bypasses, which are human-centric. It also includes concurrency issues like race conditions.

For example, Uber had a bug that allowed a user to change input in the HTTP request from "false" to "true." This allowed Uber customers to bypass built-in limits when hiring a car.

> **The Human Wins**
>
> ✓ Business Logic Bypasses
> ✓ Race Conditions
> ✓ Chained Exploits

Big vs. Small

Overall, we see that machines win when categorizing small, granular things. Humans win when thinking strategically and creatively, or "thinking big." Humans are good at thinking about the overall workflows and user journeys of an application.

Humans also shine when thinking about race conditions. For example, at Shopify, hackers figured out how to bypass a partner email confirmation so that they could take over any store. They did this by quickly modifying a resource in between the time a file is opened and the time it is processed.

One may think that scanners would be good at detecting these sorts of conditions, but multi-step workflows turn out to be a hindrance for them.

As another example of humans thinking big in order to exploit bugs, we can look at chained exploits. This is where we can use one vulnerability to find another. Using Shopify as an example again, someone was able to use server-side request forgery to get root access to all instances of the application, letting them build in other vulnerabilities on the server.

It's Not a Competition

There are certain things machines are good at and others that humans are good at. This is not a competition. We humans should be working with machines to find vulnerabilities together. Humans assisted by machines allow us to enter a new frontier where we can lean on tools while leveraging our creativity.

Takeaways

The key takeaways for all this are:

▶ Tool price is not correlated to tool quality.

▶ Creativity, not narrow thinking, is key to be better at finding vulnerabilities.

▶ Humans should work with machines instead of against them.

Remember these points and you'll excel at discovering application vulnerabilities. ∎

ABOUT THE PRESENTER

Vanessa Sauter is a security strategy analyst at Cobalt.io, a Pentest as a Service company. She previously worked at the Brookings Institution and the Aspen Institute in Washington, D.C., where she specialized in cybersecurity policy and national security law. Her interest in vulnerabilities stems from her work researching and writing about APTs for numerous publications. Vanessa graduated from Columbia University in 2016 and worked at Columbia's Graduate School of Journalism for three years.

Summary provided by Mark Henke.

Go to bit.ly/2020addo-sauter *to watch the entire presentation.*

CI/CD Pipelines for DevSecOps With Hybrid Cloud

presented by Michael Fraser

CHAPTER 31

CI/CD Pipelines for DevSecOps With Hybrid Cloud

With traditional IT, we have built everything around racking and stacking infrastructure and then deploying infrastructure. It's been project-based and uses the waterfall approach. Unfortunately, we haven't been able to apply much automation to this traditional IT infrastructure through CI/CD pipelines.

To sum up the life cycle, in the traditional IT model, we procure, pre-configure, rack, and stack, and then we do the final configuration for infrastructure.

Now, traditional IT is seen as legacy. But even though it's legacy, we need to apply automation if we want to be agile. Refactr's solution is IT-as-Code; their focus is on using tools and automation as well as changing the culture to an agile organization. With this methodology, IT becomes IT-as-Code, and everything becomes software.

The Solution: IT-as-Code

In the traditional IT model, we need to realize that resistance is futile and we must automate. So, IT-as-Code requires DevSecOps. DevSecOps adds agile infrastructure as code to agile software development.

This allows you to iterate quickly, whether it's your infrastructure, application, or your security. Everything becomes code.

How DevSecOps Fits in IT-as-Code

DevSecOps is very promising. It provides not just an automated workflow but also an automated workflow with baked in security. This workflow allows the organization to securely bring services to their customers, iteratively and continuously.

The goal is to automate as much as possible, the outcome of this is a reduction in errors caused by manual configuration. DevSecOps also automates responses to alerts and events, which again reduces errors and manual labor while increasing response speed exponentially. Finally, DevSecOps enforces security programmatically instead of manually; security will never again be an afterthought.

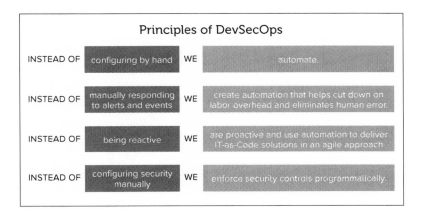

From an IT-as-Code standpoint, as we create the pipelines in an as-a-service fashion, we move from manual to automated solutions. So, we use tools like Terraform, Jenkins, etc. As we bring these tools in, we move towards a continuous process.

There are four main requirements in a CI/CD pipeline:

1. Automation
2. Integration
3. Agile delivery
4. Security

Meeting these requirements helps bring automation and agility to the organization.

How Do I Implement a DevSecOps CI/CD Pipeline?

Does this all sound easy? At a high level, yes. But how do you get there, and what does it look like with a DevSecOps CI/CD pipeline?

In this DevSecOps Reference Architecture, you can see how complicated DevSecOps can get:

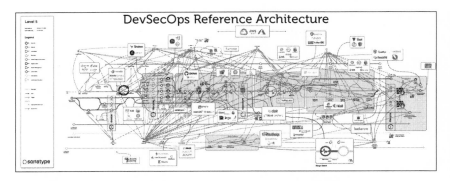

Depending on what you use, you may add four or five tools. Some organizations are using 10 to 15 tools in the pipeline to get the results they want. Suffice it to say that things can get complicated.

Let's see how, for example, DoD architecture might look with DevSecOps.

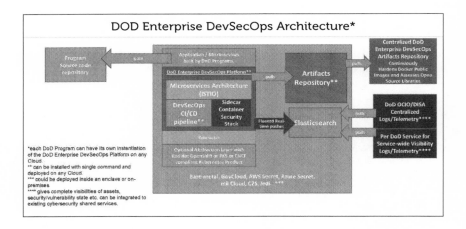

Looking at the DoD architecture, we still pull in a lot of different tools to automate and cover all our bases.

As you can see, DevSecOps is complicated, and it's an ongoing and dynamic process. You're not only configuring your CI/CD pipeline, but you're also looking ahead at new tools and services and deciding what you should be doing next.

Let's simplify this view by focusing specifically on security.

A Closer Look at Security

If we hone in on security, there's still a lot of tools. From key management, compliance, and governance to analysis, security touches everything.

Another way to look at this is to look at the technology stack for DevSecOps. In the stack, five main components provide a solid base:

▶ Infrastructure as code

▶ Configuration management

▶ API integrations

▶ Security as code

▶ Source control

Each component of this technology stack has different needs; you need to choose the appropriate tools to address these needs.

Moving onto continuous monitoring, we need tools for several layers.

▶ Application layer

▶ Service mesh layer

▶ CI/CD layer

▶ Platform layer

▶ Infrastructure layer

With so many layers, you can see why it's essential to have multiple teams and engineers involved. Again, different tools exist for each of those layers. You can chain these tools together to streamline your CI/CD pipeline.

Here's an example of a DevSecOps CI/CD pipeline and the tools you might include in it:

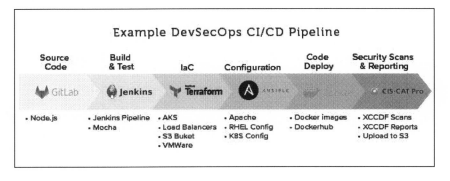

Long term, you can also look at how you can pull these components and build different pipelines for different needs. This helps create purpose-built pipelines that can be decoupled in a hybrid approach no matter where you're going to apply the pipeline.

Hybrid Architecture

When looking at a hybrid architecture, you can have a combination of on-premise environments and cloud environments. You have the same opportunities to use the tools discussed above.

Final Thoughts

In the future, software will define everything we build. Today, not everything can be built into a pipeline, but over time you'll replace components you can't automate with components that you can automate. So, even as you're moving to the cloud in a hybrid approach, look for opportunities to automate where you can.

As with most things, don't forget culture. Changing the culture of the organization, from the business side to the technical side, will increase agility for all. ∎

ABOUT THE PRESENTER

Michael Fraser is currently Co-Founder, CEO, and Chief Architect at Refactr, Inc, a firm he co-founded in 2017. Michael also worked at Optiv and Fishtech as a Cloud Security Solutions Architect for many Fortune 100 companies. Starting his career in the United States Air Force in cybersecurity, Michael left after 9 years to become an expert in DevSecOps and security automation. Michael has published many feature articles including in *Redmond Channel Partners*, featured on the cover of *Channel Pro Magazine* and has presented at numerous industry events, including: CRN, various Microsoft events, RedHat AnsibleFest, DevOps Days, and All Day DevOps. Academically, Michael earned a Master of Computer Science at Seattle University in June 2019 and is also an adjunct professor at Seattle Central College, teaching courses in Cloud, Cybersecurity and DevOps. Michael is an avid snowboarder and loves Crossfit. Finally, Michael aspires to be the world's coolest dad for his 5-year-old autistic daughter, and in his spare time creating an Augmented Reality app to help autistic children communicate better in social situations.

Summary provided by Sylvia Fronczak.

Go to bit.ly/2020addo-fraser *to watch the entire presentation.*

CHAPTER 32

Everyone's WFH
What Does That Mean for No Pants DevSecOps?

presented by Caroline Wong

CHAPTER 32

Everyone's WFH
What Does That Mean for No Pants DevSecOps?

Working from home means more than only worrying about what shirt you wear for video conferences. It also changes how we lead. There are critical changes that need to happen in order to keep organizations secure, safe, and healthy after shifting to a remote workforce. In order to keep continuity, we need to lead as a team.

Recognize Potential Points of Failure

Part of keeping everyone safe is planning for failures. This means recognizing the points of failure and making contingency plans. One of the most important steps in creating any disaster recovery plan is cataloging your software. Your software should be cataloged along with criticality and contingency plans in order to keep the business alive.

Increase Awareness

Part of keeping everyone safe is making sure they're well. When people get stressed, they might make decisions without thinking things through. In this state, they might click nefarious links in emails, get goaded into a battle with a customer, or even fall prey to bad actors. Making sure people are well is as important as keeping the technology in shape.

Be Aware of Surroundings

Any time you're working in an environment with other people, you should be sure to take certain security precautions. Locking your laptop screen before walking away, for example, is the best way to make sure your dog or child doesn't accidentally wreak havoc on your work.

Keep Current

It's as important to use secure passwords as it is to use safe internet protocols. WPA2 and closed SSID broadcasting are essential to protecting sensitive work information when working from home, but they are things that most people might need a little help to understand. Be there for them, and make sure to keep people aware of the latest protocols and how to ensure they're meeting the current standards.

Also, be sure to update your software and OS in order to keep up with the latest security patches. Most good software will also add features that will make your experience better in addition to safer. The best practice for organizations is to use management tools to keep everyone's computer up to date. However, not every company has the capability to do this. Keeping employees informed about updating software and providing support for doing the updates is better than nothing.

Strategic Takeaways

It's a brave new world out there. In this world of change and remote working, few things are certain. What we can be sure of is that people will continue to learn and grow. Although it may look different in the future, keeping people safe, secure, and healthy is as important as ever. The strategies laid out by Caroline Wong are designed to help organizations around the world do just that! ∎

ABOUT THE PRESENTER

Caroline Wong is the Chief Security Strategist at Cobalt.io. Her close and practical information security knowledge stems from broad experience as a Cigital consultant, a Symantec product manager, and day-to-day leadership roles at eBay and Zynga. She is a well-known thought leader and has contributed content to LinkedIn Learning and *Forbes*. Caroline has been featured in multiple Women in IT Security issues of *SC Magazine* and was named one of the Top Women in Cloud by CloudNOW. She received a Women of Influence Award in the One to Watch category and authored the popular textbook *Security Metrics: A Beginner's Guide*, published by McGraw-Hill. Caroline graduated from U.C. Berkeley with a B.S. in Electrical Engineering and Computer Sciences and holds a certificate in Finance and Accounting from Stanford University Graduate School of Business.

Summary provided by Sylvia Fronczak.

Go to bit.ly/2020addo-wong *to watch the entire presentation.*

CHAPTER 33

Your Kernel and You
How cgroups Make Containers Possible

presented by Marc Cluet

CHAPTER 33

Your Kernel and You
How cgroups Make Containers Possible

A quick history of containers: Containers are not actually new. They have a rich history with Unix that started in 1979. They evolved heavily in the early 2000s with FreeBSD and Solaris. Google integrated cgroups in the Linux kernel in 2006, cgroups was part of their Borg infrastructure, an app clustering system that is a spiritual precursor to Kubernetes.

At first, we only had lxc for command line support for cgroups. Then Docker came along to make it easier to work with cgroups.

What We Need for Containers

In order to have containers, we need a few things:

▶ **Isolated filesystem:** This ensures one service does not override or delete another service's data.

▶ **Isolated memory:** This helps us avoid leaks or one service accidentally starving another service.

▶ **Isolated CPU:** Similar to memory, this ensures every service has enough CPU to perform the calculations they need.

▶ **Isolated users:** This ensures every service can be secure and that data won't leak out inappropriately.

▶ **Isolated network:** This ensures each service can have stable traffic to and from the outside world.

▶ **Resource limiting:** This ensures every service has what it needs to get its job done.

▶ **Accounting and calculating consumption:** This lets the infrastructure make changes to containers as necessary to scale a service appropriately.

To achieve this, we have different namespaces in a Unix kernel:

▶ **Mount:** This lets us isolate filesystems.

▶ **UTS:** This is a special namespace because in Unix. Everything is a file and is heavily tied to the hostname. UTS lets us isolate network calls and put multiple hostnames on one server.

▶ **IPC:** This lets us isolate a subset of network calls with multiple hostnames.

▶ **PID:** This lets us isolate memory by having isolated process IDs (PIDs)

▶ **User:** This namespace lets us isolate users and groups inside the container.

▶ **Cgroup:** This is the main tool for isolation and gives us accounting and control. We can use cgroups to measure consumption and limit resources.

▶ **Time:** This lets us manage time in an isolated manner (still not implemented).

▶ **Syslog:** This lets us have multiple "server logs" in one server (still not implemented).

Not only do we have a plethora of namespaces to leverage, but they are composable. We can have namespaces mounting the same namespaces inside.

Cgroups: A Brief History

As seen above, cgroups is a namespace, most people call all namespaces cgroups even if that's not true. The use of their name has evolved, as have their features. Cgroups originally needed to be isolated per thread, and you had 12 different controls.

At the time of writing, cgroups have been around for 14 years. They needed to evolve to give us the rich functionality we see in containers today.

Cgroups version 2.0 was a complete rewrite of them. They add isolation per process, not thread, and make better use of namespaces. They could also live next to the v1 of cgroups. For example, in Bash, you can use the "cgroup2" sys filesystem reference instead of "cgroup," you can also mix and match controls from cgroup and cgroup v2.

Leveraging the Power of Cgroups

To conclude, cgroups enable an incredible array of tooling for isolating software. They are built on top of namespaces and are composable. Hopefully, this reveals some of the magic behind containers. ∎

ABOUT THE PRESENTER

Marc Cluet is the Co-Founder at Ukon Cherry, a London based consultancy specialising in DevOps. Marc has over 21 years of experience in the Industry, including companies like Rackspace, Canonical, Trainline, DevOpsGroup, Nationwide Building Society and several startups across five different countries. Marc has also spoken in some of the most prestigious conferences including FOSDEM, LISA, OpenStack Summit, UDS, Puppetconf and several meetups. Marc also is one of the organisers of London DevOps which is the second biggest DevOps meetup in the world.

Marc has contributed code to several projects including Puppet, mcollective, Juju, cloud-init and helped create MAAS. Marc loves solving complex infrastructure problems and applying solid and repeatable solutions, he is also an expert in building up agile engineering teams. You can find Mark on Twitter at @lynxman.

Summary provided by Mark Henke.

Go to bit.ly/2020addo-cluet to watch the entire presentation.

Overcoming Inertia At Scale

Moving Government to DevSecOps

presented by Amélie Koran

CHAPTER 34

Overcoming Inertia At Scale
Moving Government to DevSecOps

With some advice on how to pick projects and use metrics to incentivize employees, public sector technologists can make a successful transition to DevSecOps.

Important Differences in the Public Sector

Before we figure out how to shift the government processes to DevSecOps, we must understand the significant differences between the private and public sectors.

Public vs. Private Sector
Sisters, but not twins

Private	Public
Funding Follows Business Initiatives	Different Funding Process
Industry or Market Specific Regulations	Tighter Laws & Regulations
Both Specific and General Consumers	Everybody Is A Potential User / Customer
Legacy by Exception — Business Impact	Higher Amount Of Legacy
Modernization On-Demand / By Need	"Run The Business" vs Modernization

---

Public sector systems have different funding processes and often operate under stricter laws and regulations from private sector systems. For one thing, there is a larger amount of legacy services and technologies than in the private sector. Businesses need to aggressively modernize and possibly consolidate their legacy systems in order to stay competitive, whereas governments don't necessarily have this pressure. Additionally, in the public sector, everyone is a potential customer and user. This means a government agency has a myriad of personas they have to support and develop for, and there are known unknowns due to this situation.

The Problems

These differences can make overcoming DevSecOps inertia look like a lot of thankless work. There are issues such as:

▶ **Lots of technical, policy, and process debt.** Many legacy systems contain built-up debt to overcome. Regulation also means processes can be slow to change.

▶ **Complex politics, money and relationships.** Funding has much more oversight and process around it in government. Politics exists in the purest form of the word in the private sector, and is more based on personalities.

▶ **A lack of operational support.** Support is more important than modernization. If you build it, you will need the staff to maintain it, and public sector staff often wear "many hats" in the execution of their duties.

▶ **Contractual workforce.** Much of the public sector workforce has switched to primarily contractual in the last 20 years, with federal employees primarily focusing on project management rather than development and operations.

Risk Factors

Government technology work is inherently risky, and exists in a risk adverse environment.

It requires a significant amount of organizational cultural change. We need to support government contractors and their leads in order to succeed in introducing and continuing DevSecOps practices. As a leader, some of your key work is to get people involved, and getting employees to move from "talking about it" to "doing it."

At the same time, we need to get buy-in from leadership, business/mission areas, support staff, other public sector partners, and even external oversight and funding authorities. Buy-in is key to avoid "cost center" labels during discussions, instead aligning these efforts along CapEx and OpEx expenditure discussions. We must help federal agency workers see that technology is an enabler of public value.

Moving From Inertia

To overcome these challenges and risks, we have to follow Newton's First Law, which states that an object in motion stays in motion. This means some of the most critical steps must be followed up by a lightweight process to keep everybody rolling toward DevSecOps. Get the right people involved upfront with a consistent schedule for your initiative.

You also need to make your measurements meaningful. To incentivize people to succeed, you need measurements that point to that success and ways that they can achieve it. Make them realistic and understandable.

Too many measurements will be like trying to drink from a firehose for your employees and contractors: they won't be able to take it all in, and will likely be overwhelmed by the flow of data. Several garden hoses on a fire could be just as effective as a firehose, and allow for easier consumption and management of the data and information to be consumed.

Pick your sources of data by how useful they are and compare them to get an idea of their quality. Don't let the magnitude of the measurements overwhelm you. Remember that moving from 0 to 1 is as critical as moving from 1 to 100. Once the process is moving forward, it's a lot easier to keep it rolling than getting it started. The hardest work is the start and establishment and methods of measure, especially if they didn't formally exist prior.

How to Successfully Start Your Transition to DevSecOps

Critical to starting an effort to overcome organizational inertia with modernization and transformation activities is to pick the right projects and people. Look for projects that are well-documented and are properly resourced. Poorly resourced, managed and designed projects with very little funding are set up for failure no matter what initiative you choose, it is important to review the whole strategy for an activity and perform a gap analysis in order to identify chances for success. You will also want to select ones that are as apolitical as possible so they can be resilient to administration changes and divisive politics that typically accompany projects in any level of the public sector.

Conclusion

The work may seem tough, at times overwhelming and thankless, but, like a boulder, automobile or any seemingly large and immovable object, once it starts rolling it is easier to keep it rolling and picking up speed and velocity. Don't let any vanity or ego get in the way as it serves no appreciable purpose. Select projects that are well-documented and have the resources to support your efforts. Find people with good ideas for positive change, and support them. With perseverance and good incentives, you can make a difference in your government. ∎

ABOUT THE PRESENTER

Amélie E. Koran is currently the Senior Technology Advocate for Splunk and recently served as the Deputy Chief Information Officer and most recently as Chief Technology Officer for the U.S. Department of Health and Human Services, Office of the Inspector General. However, Amélie's path prior to today took her the long way around — through multiple industry sectors, academia, and the public sector. Her professional experience includes time spent at The Walt Disney Company, Carnegie Mellon University's CERT/CC, Mandiant, The World Bank, Constellation Energy (now Exelon) and The American Chemical Society. She began her time in the public sector as Lead Enterprise Security Architect for the U.S. Department of the Interior, eventually moving on to lead Continuous Diagnostics and Mitigation implementation for the U.S. Treasury Department. Amélie later spent time on a leadership development rotation as part of the President's Management Council Fellowship serving the Federal CIO in supporting cybersecurity policy analysis and legislative review, where she took an active role in the government-wide Open Data Initiative and helped in giving "birth" to the United States Digital Service (USDS). She's an ardent advocate for innovative approaches to hiring talent and rationally applying security strategies and technologies for the public and private sector.

Summary provided by Mark Henke.

Go to bit.ly/2020addo-koran *to watch the entire presentation.*

CHAPTER 35

Innersource for Your Enterprise

presented by Jessi Moths

CHAPTER 35

Innersource for Your Enterprise

First, let's define innersource: It is the application of open source principles to enterprise development.

The open-source community and enterprise teams face common challenges. By looking at how open-source successfully tackles these challenges, we can apply them to our enterprise.

Here are some of those challenges:

▶ **Collaboration among teams, especially distributed ones.** The current climate has emphasized how challenging working remotely can be.

▶ **Ownership and maintenance.** Open source has to deal with challenges of multi-year ownership of applications, long after the bulk of features have been written.

▶ **Rapid delivery.** Open source reacts fast to the needs of its users and develops trust with its user base.

Goals of Innersource

Innersource has four goals:

▶ **Reuse.** We want to leverage the efforts of other people so we can save time and effort for our team.

▶ **Collaboration.** When working together, we want to play to our strengths and write better software as a result.

▶ **Community.** We should understand that we are part of a larger community — a community of both our coworkers and our users.

▶ **Better, faster software.** We can ship our software frequently without lowering quality. In fact, faster feedback can increase the quality of our software.

All of this leads to overall better quality software and happier team members.

Attributes of Innersource in Action

There are five attributes of innersource in action that are worth calling out:

▶ **Openness.** We should be open with our information and our work, and we should not hoard knowledge. This should be a default paradigm, but that doesn't mean just anyone can commit to any codebase in your company.

▶ **Transparent.** We should make as much of our information as documented as possible. We should also iterate on it to ensure that it's accurate. This documentation should be preserved and open, and it also should be searchable and discoverable. Collaboration does not need to wait for approvals — let it happen while in the stream of development.

▶ **Participatory.** We want people outside our team to be able to collaborate with us. This especially includes users. They can give us rich, early feedback if we include them in our process.

▶ **Collaborative.** We want to work with people, not compete against them. Incentives should be team-focused, not individual-focused. Use teams to facilitate communication, not only structure. You should feel free to pull in experts on differing subjects, like JavaScript or security.

▶ **Governed.** Though teams should have a high level of autonomy, this isn't the Wild West. Our teams should be accountable for the things we own. There should be some level of governance that limits how we operate. This includes tools and best practices that help us follow the best paths to deliver software. Don't assume everyone knows the best way to get things done. Make it clear what you believe are the best choices for your team. Also, use guardrails, not stop signs. Don't necessarily have code reviews that stop code from being deployed, but raise signals that you can discuss as a team. Automate your governance where possible. Automated governance will not get in your way.

These attributes of innersource can tackle many of the challenges of communication in enterprise, which can be some of the most difficult ones to solve. You have to speak to people all across the organization to get your work done sometimes. Open source has to model communication in small places in order to succeed, and innersource will help us shore up our communication.

Manage Your Information

Doing all these things can result in a massive buildup of information. You must curate all of it. Consider these attributes as defaults, not rule of law. And be open with each other, free to suggest changes to improve your quality.

You'll also want to have a single source of truth for your information in order to promote discovery. Information is useless overhead if no one can find it. This doesn't mean you have to use one platform across your enterprise, but you should centralize as much as possible.

Remember to design for reuse. Find ways to ensure your information can be reused across many different scenarios. For example, you can link to your business glossary in your wiki from a user story and from a slide deck during a demo.

Next up, keep in mind that documentation is part of your software. It should be part of your day-to-day work, alongside your code. By continually working on it, you will keep the effort needed to maintain it as low as possible while keeping its accuracy high.

Finally, keep friction low for people to contribute to your documentation. For example, don't require specific team membership for coworkers from other teams to edit your wiki.

Better, Collaborative Software

By innersourcing our team, we can have effective communication, documentation, and collaboration in our enterprise. Make your processes as open and documented as possible. Keep everything as centralized and friction-free as possible.

In the end, innersourcing will enable you to have a strong, creative team able to create effective software, even in large organizations ∎

ABOUT THE PRESENTER

Jessi Moths is a Solutions Engineer at GitHub and is based in Chicago, Illinois.

Summary provided by Mark Henke.

Go to bit.ly/2020addo-moths to watch the entire presentation.

DevOps Metrics
Measuring What Matters

presented by Vlakto Ivanovski

CHAPTER 36

DevOps Metrics
Measuring What Matters

Sooner rather than later, all software development teams have to implement strong DevOps. As the product scales, the development process should get more efficient, with shorter cycles of putting high-quality software in the end user's hands. But this requires stronger collaboration between software development (Dev) and IT operations (Ops). Hence, DevOps is about applying principles and methods to improve this collaboration to build, test, and release software much faster.

Benefits of DevOps

There are various benefits to DevOps in the software development life cycle:

- **Gain a competitive advantage:** You get a competitive advantage by responding faster to business demands. A DevOps system will help you get new features to market before your competitors.

- **Increase IT resource efficiency:** You need to automate multiple deployment processes and remove manual processes. This will improve the development efficiency.

- **Enable better and faster decisions:** You can enable faster decisions by creating feedback loops. This will help identify issues as early as possible.

- **Keep pace with business demands:** Today's dynamic market leads to ever-changing requirements. A sound DevOps system helps push new updates and applications to the market faster to increase customer satisfaction.

Implementing DevOps

As discussed above, there are various benefits to implementing DevOps. However, achieving high levels of collaboration between your teams to achieve an efficient DevOps process is challenging. So, you need to address the issue in a systematic manner. First, you must assess your overall DevOps strategy to prioritize the key areas. Next, you need to identify the DevOps maturity of your development and IT operation processes. You can use the chart below to help with this. Next, you can come up with ideas on what to improve. Finally, you can implement your ideas to improve your development speed.

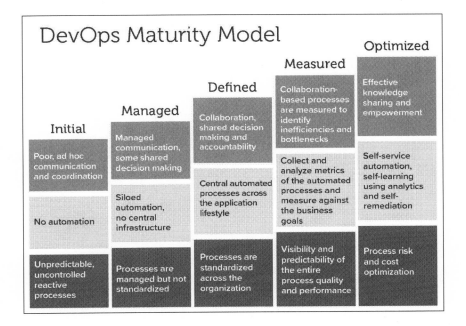

However, as Peter Drucker says, "If you can't measure it, you can't improve it." You need to constantly measure your DevOps metrics and continuously improve the processes. The process of measuring also removes subjectivity, creates predictability, and improves excellence.

What Metrics to Measure?

The key principle of DevOps metrics is to quantify a faster cadence (efficiency) and value addition (effectiveness). Some key metrics that give insights about a software development process.

LEAD TIME

The time between receiving the customer's request and delivering on that request. The code deployment lead time can usually be divided into two value streams: (1) design and development and (2) testing and operations.

PROCESS/CYCLE TIME

The time between commencement of a process and its completion for the next downstream customer.

WAIT/QUEUE TIME

The "non-value-adding" process time, wherein the process is idle and waits for the next step.

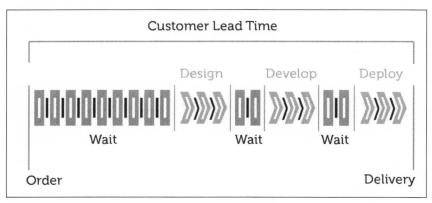

Lead time is the sum of process times plus the queue times.

WORK IN PROCESS (WIP)

The amount of work that has been started but not yet completed. A similar amount of incoming work requests and outgoing work requests allows the teams to balance their workloads.

THROUGHPUT RATE

The average number of units produced per unit time. For DevOps Kanban, you can use, for example, "user stories per day."

Process Optimization

Once the above-mentioned metrics are measured, you can create a structured visualization of the process called the *value stream map*. Value stream mapping will help your team understand where the actual value is being added in the process. This will allow you to optimize the process and improve software development efficiency. As shown below, you need to break your development cycle processes into smaller subprocesses and idle times. As you drill further, you'll discover more bottlenecks, idle times, and subprocesses.

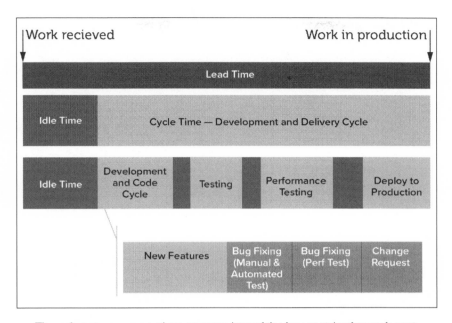

The value stream map gives an overview of the key metrics for each part. The aim of DevOps, as discussed, is to decrease the lead time. However, lead time is the sum of cycle times and idle times of the subprocesses. To decrease this lead time value, you can minimize the idle time or reduce the cycle time. For example, in the image above, the idle time before the "development code cycle" phase can be reduced by making sure the development team is ready to start work as soon as the design team is done. A higher queue or idle time reveals inefficiency in the overall process. The cycle time can be reduced by working on the process faster or using more efficient means. You need to find the cause, and a corresponding solution, for every idle time and cycle time throughout the process in the value stream map.

Conclusion

It's important to continuously measure key metrics in your DevOps process. Therefore, you need to create a value stream map, then track top metrics such as lead time, cycle time, and idle time. Moreover, you need to identify bottlenecks to make the process more efficient. ∎

ABOUT THE PRESENTER

Vlatko Ivanovski is Microsoft MVP for DevOps and ALM. Currently working as a DevOps Group Manager at Avanade, United Kingdom. With more than 17 years of IT experience and strong technical and development background he has provided a strong business foundation in Managing ICTs. He is a highly experienced DevOps & ALM professional with proven management and technical skills and demonstrates the ability to build/lead/mentor teams of other IT technical personnel in different IT functions. He is part of ALM Rangers where he continuously contributes in providing valuable extensions and guidance for Azure DevOps (Service + Server). After joining Avanade he has been part of the most complex and challenging enterprise solutions in a variety of industries (Gov, Insurance, Banking). His passion is continuously to explore and implement practices over managing the overall process of developing software solutions and delivering it using the latest technologies and techniques.

Summary provided by Aditya Khanduri.

Go to bit.ly/2020addo-ivanovski *to watch the entire presentation.*

CHAPTER 37

The Science of Compliance
Early Code to Secure Your Node

presented by Judy Johnson

CHAPTER 37

The Science of Compliance
Early Code to Secure Your Node

We're here to talk about the science of compliance. By the end of this chapter, you'll understand what compliance is, why it matters, and how to achieve it.

Why Does DevOps Matter?

We can sum up why DevOps matters in four basic points:

▶ Cooperation

▶ Communication

▶ Repeatability/Consistency

▶ Efficiency

Under DevOps, teams work together toward the same goal. With the help of automation and documentation, we can improve the way team members communicate. That leads to consistent and repeatable processes. Those processes, in turn, make the whole organization more efficient.

What is DevSecOps?

DevSecOps is basically DevOps plus security. This is how RedHat defines it:

DevSecOps means thinking about application and infrastructure security from the start. It also means automating some security gates to keep the DevOps workflow from slowing down. [...] However, effective DevOps security requires more than new tools — it builds on the cultural changes of DevOps to integrate the work of security teams sooner rather than later.

Here's another quote by Gene Kim:

66

In high-performing organizations, everyone within the team shares a common goal- quality, availability, and security are not the responsibility of individual departments, but are a part of everyone's job, every day.

99

In other words, DevSecOps is just making security a priority from the start and the responsibility of everyone.

Is the "Sec" in DevSecOps Really Needed?

Should the "Sec" part be needed in DevSecOps? Shouldn't it be implicit?

As far as I'm concerned, we should just call it "DevOps." DevOps is DevOps, it just means "we're working together, toward the same goal." If we were to add every essential or important activity that happens during the SDLC, we might as well call it "DevSecCodeTestRunDeployEtcOps" or something to that effect.

What Is Compliance? How Does it Differ From Security?

People often ask "what's the difference between security and compliance?"

Security is trying to make sure your system isn't vulnerable. Security is *disprovable*, but it's not *provable*. What does that mean?

It means that while you can't prove that a given information system is secure, you can disprove it. After all, that's what invaders do when they break into a system.

Compliance, on the other hand, is both *provable* and *disprovable*. It's a checklist or set of rules, and you can go through your tests in order to prove you're compliant.

Both security and compliance are attempts to minimize risk.

Why Do We Need Compliance?

We've just seen how compliance is different from security. But why do we need it?

The short answer would be "consistency." When you have several parties working towards the same goal, it's hard to remain consistent across the board. Having checklists, guidelines or rules for everyone to follow helps with that.

Once you accomplish consistency in a process, a number of other benefits follow. Below is a list with some of the most important reasons why an organization needs compliance:

▶ Improve security

▶ Implement security concepts in a provable way

▶ Maintain trust/integrity

▶ Maintain consistency (process management)

▶ Keep control

Ensuring Your Systems Are Compliant

To ensure your systems are compliant, you must focus on all environments: development, testing, and production.

When it comes to the development environment, the best course of action is to eliminate some of the threats — such as ports or encryption — right away. What about testing? Here, we're talking mainly about your testing framework and platform (CI). Here are the tips: make sure you test under varying conditions, don't forget to test all components together and finally, bear in mind that that's your last chance to catch issues before code goes live.

Last but not least, production. Even though your code is already live, you still have options, such as "ChaosMonkey"-like tools that randomly test for various issues, and things like canary deployments, which allow you to deploy to a small portion of the userbase, so you can easily roll back if something goes wrong.

Testing and Correction

When you're adding compliance to testing, you also have several tools at your disposal:

▶ Acceptance tests — Beaker/VM/Container tests

▶ Chef Inspec

▶ Manual testing

▶ Static code analysis tools

But the most important thing is to use the tools you already have, in order to make your testing easy and worthwhile.

Finally, for correction, there are several tools at your disposal, such as Puppet, Salt, Ansible or Chef. Additionally, you can use any programming language you already know, as well as performing corrections manually.

Summary

Before we part ways, here's a quick summary of all we've just seen:

▶ A secure OS on development and all other platforms allows you to start with an advantage.

▶ Compliance testing can — and should — be done at all stages of your CI process. Watch your test tool — there can be false positives as well as false negatives.

▶ A tool such as Puppet or Cron can run (or run scripts) at regular time increments to check your compliance, and alert you if something needs correction.

▶ Corrections can be done with an automated tool or manually.

▶ Ensure that security is integrated into your team and process. ■

ABOUT THE PRESENTER

Judy Johnson has been a software engineer for [many] years, and has been at Onyx Point since 2015. She has also functioned as a Systems Engineer, Project Manager, ScrumMaster, and a record store clerk. She was lucky enough to have started programming in the 19XXes when her Dad brought home a PDP-8. When not at work, Judy can be found baking treats, attending hockey games and rock concerts, or trying to finish a good book. Judy also loves to volunteer, especially in events that promote diversity in tech. Proof of her dedication to this cause is the fact that both of her awesome daughters are engineers.

Summary provided by Carlos Schults.

Go to bit.ly/2020addo-johnson *to watch the entire presentation.*

Getting Your Security Program to Shift Left
Operationalizing Security Controls Via DevSecOps

presented by Tony UcedaVélez

CHAPTER 38

Getting Your Security Program to Shift Left

Operationalizing Security Controls Via DevSecOps

DevSecOps is a hot topic. It's touted as a utopia where automation saves time and money while cutting risk and reducing dependencies. In reality, without effective oversight, DevSecOps leaves orphaned technologies, unmaintained repositories and application artifacts, and ruined credibility in its wake.

The value of DevSecOps lies in shifting your security program to the left in your schedule — in other words, shifting it earlier into the software development life cycle and testing against it all the time.

The Goals of DevSecOps

The high-level goals of a DevSecOps program are:

▸ Reduce security control gaps.

▸ Lessen the time spent on manual configurations.

▸ Improve incident recovery efforts.

▸ Increase security assurance across environments.

▸ Build security requirements into products and platforms.

▸ Eliminate vulnerabilities in the deployment pipeline itself.

▸ Put governance into operation.

Two of the most important aspects of DevSecOps are assurance and compliance.

ASSURANCE

Assurance ultimately dictates the reputation of any product you sell. To manage it properly, build it into your code base, infrastructure, and even the actors in your pipeline.

COMPLIANCE

Including governance in the DevSecOps process is key from a compliance point of view. By doing so, you can demonstrate compliance on an ongoing basis across all environments.

Governance currently sits outside of DevOps and catches issues too late. Instead, determine your security requirements before development starts. To do so, work with your compliance team to understand the controls they need and account for them early in the process.

Planning the Shift

The goals of shifting security left are:

▶ Ensure that all environments — not just production — receive security configuration.

▶ Reduce security and privacy discrepancies across environments.

▶ Operationalize security efforts through code and the CI/CD process.

Shifting left means not waiting until deployment time to worry about security. Instead, put security and compliance into the pipeline before any development begins, and verify it in all environments. As a result, you'll have consistency in controls across environments.

LAYERS OF NEED

The layers of need give you three ways to think about security in the pipeline: assurance; governance and compliance; and security testing. Assurance certifies your platform and environment and validates third-party libraries. Governance and compliance aligns your security controls with regulatory requirements and pulls them earlier into the pipeline. Last, test new features for security on an incremental basis, just as you do with your functional testing.

GETTING STARTED WITH DEVSECOPS

Where do you want to start? Ask yourself this question before embarking on a DevSecOps program. For example, quality of code may be your biggest risk. In that case, bring in static code analysis tools, and set them up to run in the pipeline during builds. Instead of having to bolt security on at the end, you're building a better picture of your code the entire time. Then you can put in a program to remedy any existing production issues while preventing new ones.

THREAT MODELING

Look at your entire pipeline, and apply risk to it to produce a threat model to drive your automation priorities. For example, suppose you have a financial application that traders on international exchanges use. Continuity and availability are key, and a threat model should lay out risks to each of those. In this case, availability means finding weaknesses to denial of service attacks and mitigating them across the application, stack, and infrastructure. And here's a second example: GDPR regulations require protection of certain personal information. To obey these regulations, apply threat modeling to identify noncompliance risks and to demonstrate proper controls throughout the pipeline.

Let's discuss automation further.

Automation Cases

Map your automation opportunities into your software development life cycle. For example, if your control is "Use cryptographic controls to protect your information," then there are lots of ways to comply with that across a variety of situations. Regardless, though, rely on automation and tooling to automate those checks throughout your ecosystem. Then have the findings of all automation checks saved to a repository or other source. Last, link the findings to a central website or dashboard. When auditors come, start them there to save time and staff effort.

Moving Forward

Start small and go from there. At first, let your strategy dictate your automation and priorities instead of any automation tool. Then understand the mapping between your organization's weaknesses and its threats and go from there. Last, automation should go all the way through to results analysis and remediation. ∎

ABOUT THE PRESENTER

Tony UcedaVélez is the founder and CEO of VerSprite — a global security consulting firm based in Atlanta, GA. He is also the author of Wiley's *Risk Centric Threat Modeling*, a book endorsed by the late Cyber Security Coordinator for the White House, Howard Schmidt. The book has been used in universities and enterprises worldwide as a means to apply a risk centric approach to application threat modeling. Tony has spoken at numerous OWASP, ISACA, ASIS, ISC2, ISSA, BSides conferences across four continents on the topics of cloud security, risk management, threat modeling, secure-SDLC implementation. He also has provided global training to both development groups and company executives who need to understand the impact of security programs to products and business services. Before starting VerSprite, Tony worked at various large multinational companies, some of which include GE Capital, UBS, Morgan Stanley, SunTrust Bank, Equifax, Symantec and Secureworks. Today, his organization performs varied security consulting services worldwide for both Fortune 50, global companies as well as technology startups.

Summary provided by Daniel Longest.

Go to bit.ly/2020addo-ucedavelez *to watch the entire presentation.*

CHAPTER 39

Observability Made Easy

presented by Christina Yakomin

CHAPTER 39

Observability Made Easy

When Christina Yakomin started her journey toward synthetic monitoring, she owned a platform for containerized applications and all of the underlying infrastructure. But she didn't own the applications themselves that were deployed to that infrastructure. This consisted of some application servers, cache servers, and web servers.

When she came onto the team, they had robust monitoring in place.

The Problem: Defining Healthy

But, in spite of that, it was actually pretty difficult to define what "healthy" was going to mean. For the platform, they decided to broadly consider that anything below a 500 is healthy, and that anything faster than three seconds would be a healthy response time.

They defined alerts for all of this, and everything was great... at least until she was on call for the first time. She was awakened by many calls, including false alarms.

So what gave?

Monitoring Percentages

In her case, it was that a small number of apps represented a large portion of the total traffic. So, anything happening to those apps disproportionately skewed the aggregate metrics and sent her a false alarm.

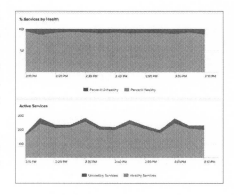

What to do? Well, next up was to monitor the percentage of healthy services.

But the false alarms continued. Why?

Well, because a small number of bad services were throwing off the service level.

Synthetic Monitoring

Next up, they decided to look into synthetic monitoring: artificially generated traffic to an application, mimicking the patterns of a typical user. This has a few advantages:

1. Traffic is controlled.

2. It complements real-traffic monitoring.

3. It mimics real user patterns.

Here was their first iteration of synthetic monitoring:

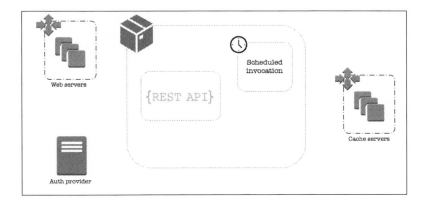

Providing this REST API for the synthetic monitoring allowed her to generate this interesting visualization of traffic through the system.

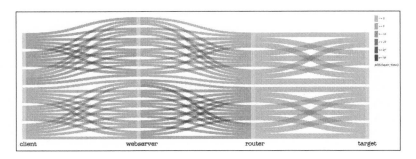

The thickness of the line represents the traffic volume flowing from point A to point B, through the system. This is a good example where the load balancer is working and the lines are even. The darkness of the line indicates latency, per the legend on the side of the screen.

So, at a glance, you can see where requests are going, how evenly, and how long it's taking. Alerts can be more sensitive while generating fewer false alarms.

However, there was a flaw. The API and the monitoring tool were in the same container. So, if anything happened to the container, it also happened to the monitoring capability.

Isolation

So she needed a layer of isolation. She needed to separate the API from the monitoring.

Here's the result of that.

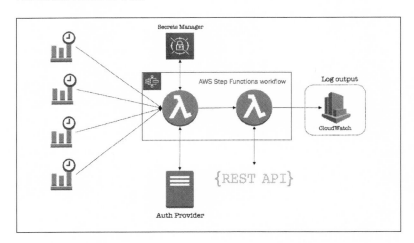

On the left are CloudWatch rules, which, on a CRON schedule invoke the state machine and go to two lambda functions. The first one talks to the secrets manager to grab credentials, and uses them to talk to the auth provider, which supplies a token. This is passed along to the second lambda function, which makes the REST request via a Python script. It makes the request and stores the results in the CloudWatch log output.

Why is this better? Well:

▶ It's isolated, so it can be available independent of the platform's availability.

▶ It's serverless, so it's cheap and even more highly available.

▶ It's global, which allows them to source their monitoring from anywhere that runs AWS Lambda, allowing for more accuracy in estimating client experience for global clientele.

So why not go with a vendor solution?

While vendor solutions are great, she already had some of the components for this in-house. And the products that she evaluated had some shortcomings, such as a lack of auth integration, expensiveness, and lockdown by a security team. With nothing ideal, and the simplicity of the Python approach, it seemed like a good idea to do it this way.

So if you find yourself in a situation like Christina's, where a vendor solution just won't work, perhaps hers can serve as the inspiration for creating what you need. ■

ABOUT THE PRESENTER

Christina Yakomin is a Site Reliability Engineer in Vanguard's Chief Technology Office. She has worked at the company's Malvern, PA headquarters since graduating from Villanova University in 2015 with an undergraduate degree in Computer Science. Throughout her career, she has developed an expansive skill set in front- and back-end web development, as well as cloud infrastructure and automation. She has earned three Amazon Web Services certifications: Solutions Architect — Associate, Developer — Associate, and SysOps Admin — Associate. Christina has also worked closely with the Women's Initiative for Leadership Success at Vanguard, both internally at the company and externally in the local community, to further the career advancement of women and girls — in particular within the tech industry. In her spare time, Christina is passionate about traveling; she has visited 20 different countries and 25 U.S. states so far! You can find Christina on Twitter at @SREChristina.

Summary provided by Erik Dietrich.

Go to bit.ly/2020addo-yakomin *to watch the entire presentation.*

Upskilling DevOps

presented by Jayne Groll

CHAPTER 40

Upskilling DevOps

There are plenty of skills that are important to have if you want high-performing DevOps in your enterprise. To help us know what those are, the DevOps Institute is here to help.

The DevOps Institute is a continuous learning community whose goal is to provide a framework of skills and ideas for advancing DevOps in the industry. Let's look at some results backed by research they've performed.

IT is a system of autonomous other systems. The various aspects of IT learning didn't start off unified. These ideas, such as scrum and continuous delivery, emerged separately. Then DevOps came along as yet another initiative: how we deal with post-production support.

The problem with these separate systems of systems is that there's no integrated way to work across our tools and teams. We need to stop the system of systems and view software delivery as part of a single value stream; we need to be thinking end-to-end about our software.

Becoming T-Shaped

In order to develop into systems thinkers, we must become T-shaped professionals. This means we have a wide breadth of knowledge but also deep knowledge in a couple of areas. For example, if we're software engineers, we need a basic knowledge of test-driven-development. A cloud engineer may need to know some Python for scripting deployments.

It's what's at the top of the T, as a T-shaped professional, that will bring your software performance to life. We need that broad knowledge to support key specialized skills for that performance. This includes soft skills.

The Skills You Need

The DevOps Institute partnered with Chief Research Analyst Eveline Oehlrich to ask what software skills are must-haves, nice-to-haves, or unimportant to software professionals across the globe. The results?

There are three key "must-have" skill categories: automation, process, and soft skills.

Automation seems obvious, but the survey showed that soft skills and technical skills are equally important. This comes from an almost equal distribution of operations professionals and software delivery professionals.

IT operations and security are also key. Everyone needs to understand their software development lifecycle, and they ignore it at their own peril.

But the biggest takeaway is this: organizations must recognize that hiring from within is key to high performance. They need to upskill those employees to meet new roles.

But Which Skills Are Most Important?

According to the DevOps Institute's research, depending on the role of survey respondents, there were different perspectives. The C-suite valued automation and soft skills the most. Managers put importance evenly across process, automation, and soft skills. Individual contributors thought automation and process skills were must-haves, with soft skills closely behind in importance.

Interestingly, all three groups rated process skills equally. It seems to be universally understood that all roles need to grasp the processes in which they participate.

Breaking down functional skills, we see that IT operations knowledge was considered the most important one. Even if not directly involved, software professionals need to understand how their software works in production.

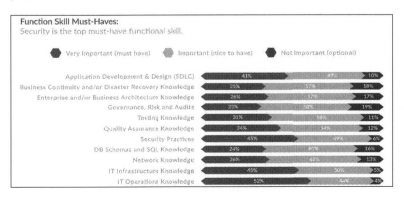

What else is valuable to those polled? Security practices were at the top. We professionals are increasingly aware of security's critical role.

As far as technical skills, we need to understand that cloud reigns over everything else. This will be key for us if we want to handle the complexity that our systems contain. Trailing far behind knowledge of the cloud are a few things, like:

▶ Knowledge of specific frameworks

▶ Experience with UI design

▶ Mobile environment knowledge

Software professionals are gaining an understanding of how important it is to create a healthy user experience.

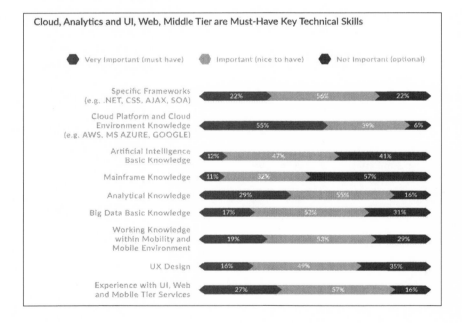

With process skills, understanding your software development lifecycle leads the way in importance, but just by a little bit. We must know how software is incepted, implemented, put into production, and used.

We also need to track and understand this flow: not just our part in it but also the overall value stream. And it's vital to know our source control tools and processes, such as continuous integration. We need to know how this fits within the flow of our software. In IT we love our frameworks, and this shows in the bottom half of our skill breakdowns. We're not loyal to a specific framework, but it's worth knowing what framework is useful for what environments.

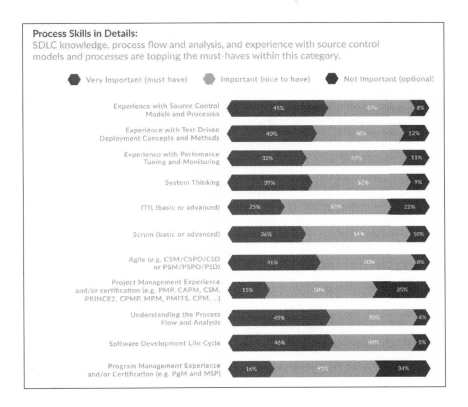

Process Skills in Details:
SDLC knowledge, process flow and analysis, and experience with source control models and processes are topping the must-haves within this category.

The Takeaway? Work on Being T-Shaped, on Your Soft Skills, and on Your Automation Skills

Soft skills, where the key is to be a good problem solver and collaborator, is almost universally understood to be of critical importance. Software is a team sport, not one of individual acumen.

Personal values are also important. We're here to improve humanity. Survey respondents seemed to understand that empathy is an important learned skill and not just something that one is born with. The message here is strong: if you're looking for a good job, you need to deliberately develop your soft skills.

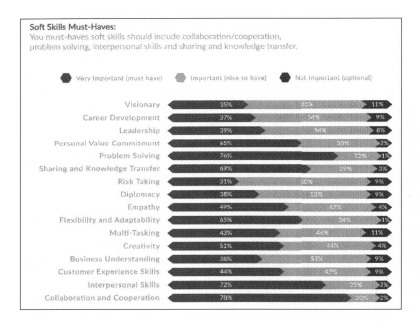

Soft Skills Must-Haves:
You must-haves soft skills should include collaboration/cooperation,
problem solving, interpersonal skills and sharing and knowledge transfer.

Skill	Very Important (must have)	Important (nice to have)	Not Important (optional)
Visionary	35%	55%	11%
Career Development	37%	54%	9%
Leadership	39%	54%	8%
Personal Value Commitment	65%	33%	2%
Problem Solving	76%	22%	1%
Sharing and Knowledge Transfer	69%	29%	3%
Risk Taking	31%	60%	9%
Diplomacy	38%	53%	9%
Empathy	49%	47%	4%
Flexibility and Adaptability	65%	34%	1%
Multi-Tasking	43%	46%	11%
Creativity	51%	44%	4%
Business Understanding	38%	53%	9%
Customer Experience Skills	44%	47%	9%
Interpersonal Skills	72%	25%	2%
Collaboration and Cooperation	78%	20%	2%

To wrap up, a final emphasis: we should become T-shaped. No matter what role we're in — whether it's security, operations, or software delivery — we must understand the breadth of skills needed across roles. We don't have to be an expert in the skills of other roles; we just need enough knowledge to be multidimensional systems thinkers.

We are all part of the same value stream. Polish your soft skills every day and keep building your automation skills. Look at recent technology, such as Kubernetes. Stay curious and be aware that your company is cultivating DevOps skills from within.

If you'd like to learn more, you can find a full copy of the report discussed here at the DevOps Institute website. ■

ABOUT THE PRESENTER

Jayne Groll is co-founder and CEO of the DevOps Institute (DOI). Her IT management career spans over 25 years of senior IT management roles across a wide range of industries. Her expertise spans multiple domains including DevOps, Agile, ITIL and Leadership. Jayne is a recognized and respected IT thought leader and influencer. In addition to authoring the Agile Service Management Guide, Jayne has co-authored several IT position papers including "Modernizing IT Operations in the Age of DevOps" that was published in 2018 by IT Revolution. Jayne is very active in the global DevOps, ITSM and Agile communities and is a frequent presenter at local, national and virtual events. You can find Jayne on Twitter at @JayneGroll.

Summary provided by Mark Henke.

Go to bit.ly/2020addo-groll *to watch the entire presentation.*

Establishing an Open Source Program Office

presented by Lee Calcote

CHAPTER 41

Establishing an Open Source Program Office

It feels like we don't have a strong understanding of open source itself. Some scars have come from working with open source in an environment filled with proprietary software. When the words "open" and "source" were brought together, there was a visceral reaction. People were skeptical of it. Some even despised it.

There's no one-size-fits-all way to bring open source into your ecosystem. But it does require a strong champion.

The Reason to Create an Open Source Program Office

Why even create an open source program office? The answer to this question depends on what kind of environment you're in. Are you in a large business? Perhaps you want one in order to increase industry influence. Or perhaps it will help increase talent.

For many organizations, it can be very much about compliance. You may be using open-source software but not sure if you're following the necessary regulations for using it.

Prominence

You may have heard of the term "software is eating the world." This means that software is touching more and more parts of all industries. In a similar way, cloud is eating the software world. Open source is touching almost every software system through cloud tooling.

Benefits

Open source programs have brought many benefits, such as:

▶ Awareness of use

▶ Development velocity

▶ Compliance

▶ Influence

Organizations with an influential open source program can attract better talent, too.

Strategy

To put together a good strategy for starting an open source program, here are 5 C's to follow:

1. **Consumption:** Getting your organization to use open source. Using open source can significantly speed up delivery. It can give you more flexibility to modify the code as you need.

2. **Compliance:** Ensuring licensing and security is compliant with regulations. Having good compliance tooling lets you deal with legal injunctions, and it can save you from customer service headaches. You can also easily deal with other risks, like intellectual property loss and engineering rework. Ensure you're tracking licenses for your open source software. Remediate vulnerabilities that pop up. Empower engineering teams to be as self-service as possible in using open source. It may be tempting to stop at compliance.

3. **Community:** Engaging with experts using open source outside your organization to help grow skills within your organization. This will gain you momentum. Be purposeful in your engagement.

4. **Contribution:** Changing the open source software you're using to make it better. To do this, you need to delineate what is and isn't IP. You need to consider all license agreements. You should also define how to govern the project.

5. **Competition:** You may actually be competing with open source software. Or perhaps you're integrating with it.

You'll want to continually ingest software from multiple sources. When using third party systems, you're likely touching open source in some way.

Role of an Open Source Program Office

By creating an open source program office, you'll be streamlining the use of open source across your organization.

Where you should build an open source program office can depend on your goals. Marketing, engineering, and operations are all potentially good departments in which to form one.

Ensure you align with your business, as well as with legal counsel, when building an open source program office. You also want to collaborate with product management to ensure you're helping your organization's products get out the door quickly.

Leveraging an open source program office will let you be in continual compliance in your DevOps pipeline.

To know you're on the right path, you want to measure your success. Try using a dashboard to look at your compliance ratings and where open source is used.

You need executive support for such an initiative. There are gaps in understanding what open source is about. You'll need to be patient and teach leadership the value an open source program office will bring.

Conclusion

Open source touches almost every aspect of software these days. Such usage may inspire a need to develop an open source program office to streamline its use and compliance. By aligning your goals with your business and using success metrics, you can make it clear the value such an office brings. ■

ABOUT THE PRESENTER

Lee Calcote is an innovative product and technology leader, passionate about developer platforms and management software for clouds, containers, functions and applications. As founder of Layer5, advanced and emerging technologies have been a consistent focus through Calcote's tenure at SolarWinds, Seagate, Cisco and Schneider Electric. An advisor, author, and speaker, he is active in the tech community as a Docker Captain and Cloud Native Ambassador., You can find Lee on Twitter at @lcalcote.

Summary provided by Mark Henke.

Go to bit.ly/2020addo-calcote *to watch the entire presentation.*

CHAPTER 42

The OWASP ZAP HUD

presented by Simon Bennetts

CHAPTER 42

The OWASP ZAP HUD

What is ZAP? ZAP (Zed Attack Proxy) is an open-source web application scanner. It's an OWASP flagship project that you can use to find vulnerabilities in a web application.

Where Can You Use ZAP?

You can use ZAP on Windows, Linux, and Mac OS. You'll have access to multiple docker images, and ZAP is suitable for beginners as well as security professionals who are working on vulnerability analysis.

You can run ZAP in desktop and daemon modes. You can also use it manually at any stage in development. It's a great tool for automated testing.

A Quick Look at ZAP

Let me show you around the ZAP tool. ZAP gives you two options: automated testing and manual testing.

AUTOMATED TESTING WITH ZAP

If you choose automated testing, you'll see this window:

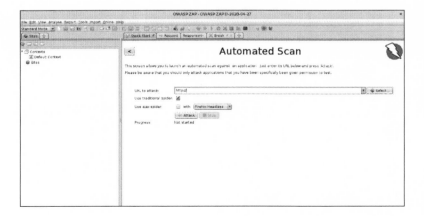

In this window, you'll have to enter the IP address of the application that you want to scan and choose the spider. Spiders are programs that crawl through the application to collect whatever information they can.

Once you click the Attack button, ZAP will spider through the web application, exploring all the links it can find. It will not only scan for vulnerabilities but will also attack the web application. Make sure you use ZAP only on the web applications you have permission to use it on, or else it'll be considered illegal.

MANUAL TESTING WITH ZAP

When it comes to manual testing, you'll have to provide the URL of the web application that you want to use ZAP on. But instead of using a spider, you'll have to manually browse through the website. ZAP will do its job only on the web pages that you manually visit.

ANALYZING RESULTS

Once you run ZAP on the application, the History tab will show you a list of all the requests made to the browser.

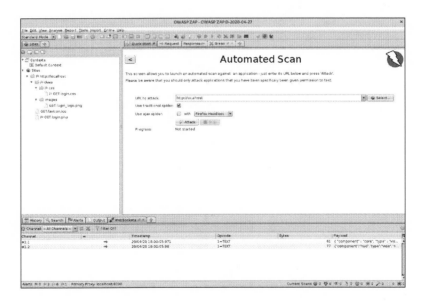

If you want to see the details of the request, click the Request tab. You'll see those details and the response under the Request and Response tabs.

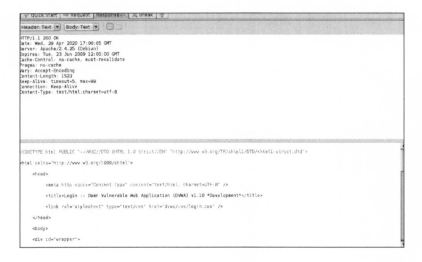

To your left, you'll see a site streak generated. This represents the way ZAP has understood your application. The site streak is really helpful when it comes to automated testing.

To find out what else you can do with the results, you can right-click on any result on the site streak.

What Is ZAP HUD?

As you can see above, using ZAP can get a little complicated for complex operations. In such cases, ZAP HUD (heads-up display) will ease things for you.

ZAP HUD lets you use the features of ZAP without having to switch to the ZAP window every time.

To use HUD, you can check the Enable HUD box while starting the session. Once you start the session, you'll see a window pop up, which means the ZAP HUD has started.

Want to learn about the ZAP HUD features? Click the Take the HUD Tutorial button, and you'll be redirected to a page with everything you need to know.

When you enable HUD, you'll see a lot of options on the left and to the right of your screen. These options lists make it easy for you to use different features of ZAP while you're using other applications or manually scanning your target.

ZAP HUD FEATURES

To your left, you'll see low, medium, and high levels of alerts. This makes it easy for you to look at the results because they're just one click away. To your right, you'll see options for site streak, spiders, and so on.

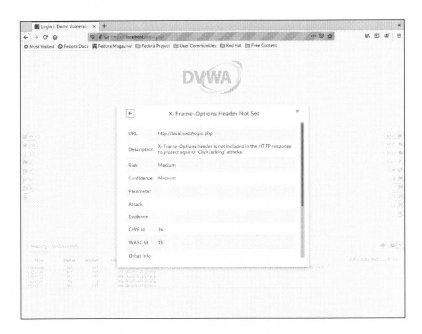

One useful feature that you may like is a button that scans for hidden fields on the page. It'll show you the number of hidden fields, and when you click it, it'll display those fields.

You can use HUD to intercept traffic, make changes to it, and pass it to the web application. It's really useful for penetration testing and debugging.

If you don't want to go around all the pages and try an exploit, you can use the attack mode. This option will automatically attack all the pages that you've added in scope.

HOW DOES ZAP HUD WORK?

Basically, ZAP stands in between your browser and the web server. HUD injects a JavaScript code in the application, which creates the frames and lets you use ZAP features.

At some point, you'll wonder, "How does ZAP HUD do all this?" Well, good news! ZAP provides the source code publicly so you can learn how the magic happens.

All right, folks! That gives you some introductory information about ZAP HUD. I suggest you install ZAP HUD (**github.com/zaproxy/zap-hud**) and explore more of its features. ∎

ABOUT THE PRESENTER

Simon Bennetts is the OWASP Zed Attack Proxy (ZAP) Project Leader and works for Mozilla as part of the Cloud Services Security Team. He has talked about and demonstrated ZAP at conferences all over the world, including Blackhat, JavaOne, FOSDEM and OWASP AppSec EU, USA & AsiaPac. Prior to making the move into security he was a developer for 25 years and strongly believes that you cannot build secure web applications without knowing how to attack them.

Summary provided by Omkar Hiremath.

Go to bit.ly/2020addo-bennetts *to watch the entire presentation.*

CHAPTER 43

Compliance as Code

presented by Gert Jan van Halem

CHAPTER 43

Compliance as Code

I f your business is regulated, you already know compliance is a must have. But how can you make it easier? In this chapter, you'll learn about compliance as code and will see an example solution that will help you verify your product's compliance.

What is Compliance?

In general, compliance means conforming to a set of rules that are set for you. As you can see, it's quite a simple concept.

But while compliance is simple, when it comes to coding products, it's also critically important — especially nowadays, with the growing number of regulations.

If you search for the word "compliance" on LinkedIn, you'll see that there's a demand for professionals that have compliance-related skills.

Why is Compliance Getting So Big? Why Do We Need All These Compliance Professionals?

A long time ago, compliance was simple. You had something that you had to bring into production, and you followed a simple set of rules. Then you delivered it, and it would get inspected.

But slowly and steadily, sometime around 2008, the rules started to grow, and the regulators kept adding to those rules.

So now you have lots of rules to keep in mind while building your product. And complying with all those rules is difficult. It's a block in the developer's way of reaching their final goal of sending the product to production.

But at the end of the day, you still need to be compliant. So developers have to follow the rules.

Awareness of Compliance

Everybody on the team understands that compliance is an important part of the product and of their jobs. They just want to be able to be compliant without a big process.

Everybody is aware of the need for compliance. But in the day-to-day, team members often just get their job done. Compliance is a lost thought in the back of their minds.

Then, around twice a year, when the product is ready to be sent into production, people start to focus on compliance, turning on their awareness of it. By then, though, it's often too late. They have to waste a sprint to get it done.

Process, Not Product

Here's another fact to take into consideration: The compliance-focused team might know everything about how the process should be done but nothing about the product itself.

It's also important to mention that not everything gets checked. When there's a number of random changes, often the compliance check happens months after the process.

So team members might assume that if there's something wrong with the process there's also something wrong with the product, and vice-versa. That's not necessarily true.

The process may have been perfect, and everything might be fine according to compliance. But that doesn't mean the end product is necessarily OK.

How to Fix This?

The folks at Gert Jan van Halem's company Devoteam knew they had to fix these problems. After some research, they found a framework called "In-Toto," created by New Jersey Institute of Technology and NYU, that could secure the integrity of software supply chains. Here's how it works.

If you look into your supply chain, there are a few steps that your product goes through. Some people are allowed to work in each step. Once step one is done, the chain moves to step two, and so on until the product is sent to production. In-Toto, the framework Devoteam adopted, helps you make checks after each step.

You start with a layout that describes the steps to take and how the process should flow. Then you actually go through the steps, following layout instructions.

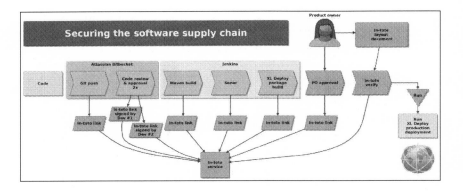

The last part of the process is the inspection. It's at this stage that you'll get back a report saying if the product is OK or not. If the product passes the inspection, it can go to production. If not, you can go back and see exactly which steps need to be worked on.

Process AND Product

If you adopt a framework like In-Toto, things get much easier. Now you check your process and your product at the same time. You describe your process in a certain way, and it's codified, so there's no misunderstanding.

Following this system means you also checked the product, making sure nothing was tampered with. You inspected it in between steps, so you're sure it works the way you expect it to. And if it doesn't, you know where the issue is. If something goes wrong, it can be fixed right away. Compliance awareness is a daily part of the routine.

Conclusion

Having a framework for compliance means a developer can actually address compliance easily and as a part of their daily job. It ensures you can bring to production a product that's compliant, that you're sure isn't tampered with, and that works as it's supposed to. ∎

ABOUT THE PRESENTER

Gert Jan van Halem is a long time Lean and Agile enthusiast. He loves to help teams and organizations to add more value to their customers. With a masters degree in Computer Science and experience as a manager, he is able to combine the hands-on implementation of automation and making sure this is embedded in the organization.

Summary provided by Pachi Carlson.

Go to bit.ly/2020addo-vanhalem *to watch the entire presentation.*

Why Manual Verification Still Matters

presented by Jeroen Willemsen

CHAPTER 44

Why Manual Verification Still Matters

I n the last few years, we've continuously been hearing that we should automate, automate, automate. So it might be weird to hear that manual verification still matters, but we still need to perform manual checks.

The Application in its Runtime

Most applications consist of application code and external libraries that are executed by a runtime:

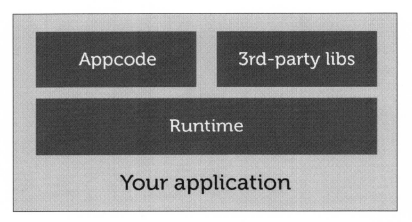

You'll potentially have issues in these places:

- ▶ third party libraries
- ▶ your application code
- ▶ your runtime

THIRD-PARTY LIBRARIES

The first thing to do is to check your dependencies manually. It's important to learn how to verify if an issue is actually a problem and how to fix it.

Fixing can mean:

▶ replacing the library

▶ marking the issue as not being a problem

▶ changing application code to deal with the vulnerability

After that, you can start automating this process. But there are caveats. For example, not all ecosystems have proper dependency checkers. And even if they do, not finding a registered vulnerability doesn't mean it's not there.

YOUR APPLICATION CODE

A great starting point for securing your application code is to use a static analysis tool, or SAST (Static Application Security Testing). The tooling here varies greatly among languages and frameworks.

When you decide to suppress warnings or errors, make sure you explain why you're doing so. This will make it clear to anyone seeing the suppression once you're no longer on the team.

If you're looking at a commercial tool, test before you buy. What works for one team, might not work for another.

But these tools will never find everything. For example, a static analysis tool won't tell you if authorization rules are set up correctly or if you're disclosing information in errors.

YOUR APPLICATION

If you want to know how your backend is behaving in general, you can use a DAST tool (Dynamic Application Security Testing). This will help you

▶ find missing headers

▶ detect some obvious missed XSS or SQL injection vulnerabilities

It will, of course, create false positives (issues that can be ignored) or false negatives (things that the tool thinks are OK but are in fact a problem).

And when you do find a vulnerability, through manual or automatic tests, you can write your own security test. You can even add "evil user stories" in your backlog. These tests will only run successfully if your application isn't vulnerable to the attack.

The Container

Basically, this is what your application in a container looks like:

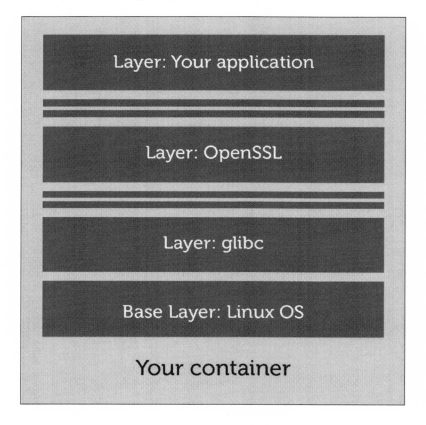

It's a bunch of layers built upon a base OS layer. At the top is your application. The layers below your application might have vulnerabilities or might be wrongly configured leading to vulnerabilities.

Some tools that can help are:

▶ Clair

▶ Anchore

▶ Lynis

- Inspec
- Dockle
- Hadolint

The Container on its Platform

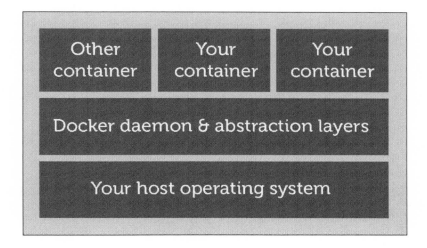

As with the previous sections, each of these blocks can have security vulnerabilities. For example, your Docker daemon might be configured in an insecure way. Or the host operating system could have security issues.

Use tools like

- Inspec
- CIS-CAT
- Lynis
- Openscap
- OpenVAS
- Nessus

In this part, immutability is king. If your systems are dynamic, you need to scan all your systems. But if you're using a fixed and immutable image, you can scan only that image. Also, the smaller the host, the smaller the attack surface.

General Issues

There are some general issues as well.

LEAKING SECRETS

One issue is that secrets may leak. You'll have to

- Scan your source code (you can do that with trufflehog)
- Check your containers (with grep and other tooling)
- Verify virtual machine images
- Check runtimes
- Check CI/CD pipelines

These are all places that might contain hard-code secrets in plain text. Be sure to also validate the process, because maybe not everyone knows how to work with secrets correctly.

NETWORK ISSUES

For the network, it's best to deny access by default. If you're in the cloud, most providers offer tooling. If you're not, use tools like nmap and checkssl.sh.

And don't forget that manual verification may still be necessary to identify unexpected infiltration or exfiltration paths.

IAM ISSUES

IAM issues can manifest themselves at different levels:

- Application
- Host
- Cloud provider

Your cloud provider should have a decent set of tools to get started. Then move up the stack. It will still require manual reviews: are the rules too broad, or too fine grained? Are our rules compliant with legal obligations?

CLOUD HOSTING CONFIGURATION ISSUES

Cloud providers have their own tooling ecosystem, so use those. But something like Cloud Custodian is "cross-cloud." If you're using Terraform, you can look at terraform-compliance.

Should You Automate?

Does this make you feel like you need to automate more? Good! Automate as much as you can. But realize that we can't catch every mistake with automation.

Also, take risk based actions. Assess the risk of what you see first, otherwise you might drown in a pool of to dos. ∎

ABOUT THE PRESENTER

Jeroen Willemsen is a Principal Security Architect at Xebia. With a love for mobile security, he recently became one of the project leaders for the OMTG project (MASVS & MSTG). Jeroen is more or less a jack of all trades with interest in infrastructure security, risk management and application security.

Summary provided by Peter Morlion.

Go to bit.ly/2020addo-willemsen *to watch the entire presentation.*

CHAPTER 45

Anatomy of a Continuous Delivery Pipeline

presented by Kamalika Majumder

CHAPTER 45

Anatomy of a Continuous Delivery Pipeline

What does a continuous delivery pipeline look like? Which pieces do we need to have in place for us to achieve true continuous delivery? Let's lay out the anatomy of a continuous delivery pipeline.

What Companies Need

Companies are always looking for

▶ Shorter release cycles

▶ Continuous integration

▶ QA

▶ Security

In essence, they want to sell faster and sell better quality products. This applies to all companies, whether they're selling services or actual products.

Most companies use many different DevOps tools, but don't have the results to show for it because:

▶ They can't deliver when they want to

▶ They encounter regression bugs in production

▶ The delivery of new features is slow

Why do we still see these issues a decade after DevOps gained traction?

One-Stop Station

Everyone needs one single pipeline for the application lifecycle management and continuous delivery of quality products. This includes:

▶ Development

▶ Testing

- ▶ Monitoring
- ▶ Release

This all needs to be linked together into one single pipeline. Today, we'll focus on the basics of a continuous delivery pipeline.

Back to Basics

Here's how Martin Fowler defined continuous delivery:

Continuous Delivery is a discipline where you build software in such a way that the software can be released to production at any time.

It's important to stress that your code is always deployable. This means continuous delivery is a cycle of five principles:

- ▶ Develop
- ▶ Build
- ▶ Test
- ▶ Deploy
- ▶ Release

Development

During development, merging code can lead to merge conflicts. This is a frustrating experience. This is caused by waiting too long to merge your changes back into the master branch. You need to keep your code updated, shortening the feedback cycle.

Trunk based development solves this issue. Temporary branches are OK for features, and short-lived release branches are fine. But everyone should commit to the master branch regularly (once a day!).

If you have unfinished code, hide it with feature toggles instead of keeping a branch open for too long.

Keep your master branch in a releasable state and never add to a broken master branch.

Build

We're still seeing "it works on my machine" issues.

We should build our artifacts once and deploy multiple times. We should version our artifacts (using semantic versioning). And this means all our artifacts: applications, configuration, database scripts, etc. Automate all of this in a pipeline.

Test

Previously, many teams built their applications first and added tests later. This leads to many manual tests and UI tests. This is a slow and error-prone process. It's better to start from the bottom up using test driven development. Write your tests first. This leads to a shorter feedback cycle.

Then work your way "up" and automate each level: integration, API and UI tests. Don't forget performance and security tests as well.

Deploy

When something in the infrastructure changes, this can break things and then we often have a hard time finding the cause. Version controlling your infrastructure as code helps identify changes that were made to the infrastructure.

This also applies to configuration. If everything is in source control, you can easily see what changed and why.

When you have infrastructure and configuration as code, you can run automated tests against it. Just like you write unit tests for your code, you can write unit tests for infrastructure or configuration.

Then we can version this and run it through a continuous integration pipeline. This way, you can link application versions and configuration versions to what is running in production.

Finally, look at zero downtime deployments. In this day and age, you should be able to update your system without downtime.

Release

Avoid having one deployment team. If your deployment pipeline is configured correctly, with the correct access rights, anyone from the development team can deploy to production.

Once you're running your application, make sure you have robust monitoring, logging and alerting:

▶ How long does it take to build?

▶ To deploy?

▶ To fix an issue?

This is useful to improve your continuous delivery cycle over time.

And always have a plan B. If something goes horribly wrong, make sure you can perform a rollback.

A Single Pipeline

Having a single pipeline to get your code to the customer is key here. Integrate often into a single master branch (or trunk) and automate the steps to get your application out there. ■

ABOUT THE PRESENTER

Kamalika Majumder helps customers in a variety of domains like Banking & Financials, Insurance, E-Commerce, and Retail achieve continuous delivery of quality products and services with faster, consistent and reliable release cycles and reduced time to Market. She has been an active practitioner of infrastructure development and DevOps disciples and through her analysis, discovery and quality engineering she helps organizations transform traditional IT to a DevOps driven lifecycle by forming cross-functional poly-skilled teams.

Summary provided by Peter Morlion.

Go to bit.ly/2020addo-majumder *to watch the entire presentation.*

CHAPTER 46

CI/CD for Serverless Applications on AWS

presented by Mohamed Labouardy

CHAPTER 46

CI/CD for Serverless Applications on AWS

A serverless architecture combined with event-driven design can reduce response time and cost. As usage grows, this architecture allows your system to grow and scale with load.

Mohamed Labouardy uses a Jenkins master with workers in an autoscaling group to deploy the serverless components. His team uses the Gitflow model as they develop AWS Lambda functions.

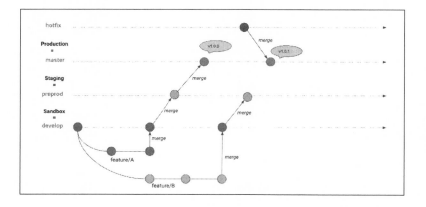

The main stages of the serverless development and CI process are the same as what you'd have in a microservices architecture. The difference lies mainly in the details. For example, Mohamed uses Docker in the build step so that he doesn't have to install dependencies on the Jenkins servers. Of course, you can take advantage of containers in many similar ways.

After the build stage, Mohamed stages artifacts (the built code) on S3 using the Git commit hash as the artifact name. This helps them keep a link between the artifact and the commit. When it's time to deploy, the AWS Lambda functions are swapped into the environment.

By the way, you don't have to use a strictly serverless architecture. You can mix and match serverless components with containerized components and even whole subsystems that run on virtual machines such as AWS EC2.

Mohamed demonstrated the whole process from a CI/CD perspective using his IMDB sample. The code for this sample is available at github. com/mlabouardy/alldaydevops-engine-2019.

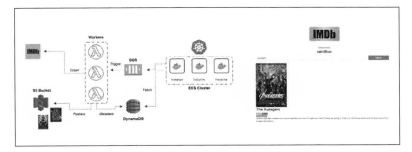

The Jenkinsfile includes many of the standard build stages as follows:

▶ Checkout

▶ Quality test

▶ Unit test

▶ Security test

▶ Build

▶ Push

▶ Deploy

The actual mechanism for swapping the Lambda lives in the Jenkins deploy stage. The Jenkins stage uses the AWS CLI to update the Lambda alias. Each Lambda can have multiple aliases, typically one for each version. You simply use the specific alias to point to the version you want to run in any environment.

With a CI/CD for a serverless architecture, you can push changes to any environment within under two minutes! Of course, results will vary with size and complexity. ■

ABOUT THE PRESENTER

Mohamed Labouardy is a Senior DevOps Manager at Foxintelligence, Founder of Komiser.io a cloud cost optimization platform. Open source contributor and Author of *Serverless Architecture in AWS with Golang*.

Summary provided by Phil Vuollet.

Go to bit.ly/2020addo-labouardy *to watch the entire presentation.*

Shifting Security Left
The Innovation of DevSecOps

presented by Tom Stiehm

CHAPTER 47

Shifting Security Left
The Innovation of DevSecOps

What is DevSecOps? It involves taking all the practices of DevOps and pulling in security practices to improve security. In DevSecOps, we want to shift security left. Shifting left brings security into the application process earlier instead of allowing it to be an afterthought.

Why Shift Security Left?

Shifting left lets us deal with security issues early and often. If we leave security practices to the end, we end up with security defects in production. So shifting left reduces risk and the costs of fixing security problems.

As with other bugs, finding and fixing security bugs earlier leads to fewer errors and fewer compromises.

How Can We Do This?

Let's next talk about how we can shift security left.

PROCESSES

We start with proactive processes instead of reactive processes. Then we architect and design security early. Finally, we automate testing that focuses on security as well.

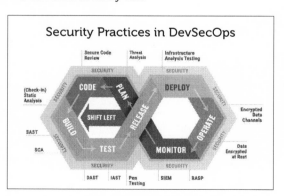

An important step is to also review the automated test results and remediate early. Without that step, we won't be fixing problems before they hit production.

SCA AND SAST

When looking at the model above, look at all the ways that you can bring security into every step. When planning, we can use threat analysis to figure out what our risks for the application are. Then when we write our code, we can use static analysis (SCA or SAST) to make sure we're not introducing vulnerabilities like SQL injection. With SAST, we're analyzing the code we've written for common vulnerabilities. On the other hand, with SCA, we're looking for vulnerabilities in our dependencies like open-source libraries. The combination of SAST and SCA will help us determine if we have something that puts us at risk.

DAST, IAST, AND PEN TESTING

Next we'll look at DAST and IAST. DAST provides dynamic testing against your running application. One problem with that seems to be a number of false positives. IAST uses an interactive model that watches your software to see if someone is currently attacking your system. It's been shown to have fewer false positives than DAST.

Another great tool is pen testing. This can be automated or manual testing against your running system.

For your production system, tools like RASP and SIEM can provide additional views of security. Again, with all these tools the focus is on bringing security into the whole development lifecycle.

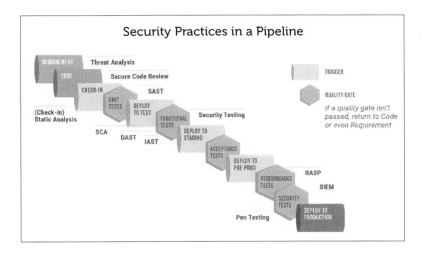

When looking at the DevOps pipeline, you can see how these tools can fit in throughout the process. As you can see, we've got a number of places where we're pulling security in. This is more thorough and reduces risk compared to the old model where we did security testing and analysis last.

Where to Start

So where should we begin? Starting with SCA provides a lot of benefits. Many vulnerabilities have been found and exploited because of open-sourced dependencies. Because teams don't always know their dependencies are vulnerable, they often have delays in getting the dependencies patched or upgraded.

The next step would be using SAST. It's quick to integrate in the build pipeline and provides benefits for the code your team writes.

And third, we can start looking at DAST. It's a bit more involved, but it's becoming more automated and easier to integrate into your pipeline.

Going back to the shifting left, let's talk about the culture shift. The culture shift should build the mindset that "everyone is responsible for security."

Part of that includes building a knowledge base. Encourage people to talk about how to deal with security challenges. Work with your security professionals to share that knowledge between teams. Figure out what lessons teams can learn from each other.

Each organization is different. We have different processes and different tools. Start doing things that work and stop doing things that don't work for your particular organization.

Starting to shift left is more important than which practices you start with. Write security requirements and make sure that you have tests that verify your security requirements are covered. And make iterative changes to improve the process. ∎

ABOUT THE PRESENTER

Tom Stiehm has been developing applications and managing software development teams for over twenty years. As CTO of Coveros, he is responsible for the oversight of all technical projects and integrating new technologies and testing practices into software development projects. Recently, Tom has been focusing on how to incorporate DevSecOps and agile best practices into projects and how to achieve a balance between team productivity and cost while mitigating project risks. One of the best risk mitigation techniques Tom has found is leveraging DevSecOps and agile testing practices into all aspects of projects. Previously, as a managing architect at Digital Focus, Thomas was involved in agile development and found that agile is the only methodology that makes the business reality of constant change central to the process. You can find Tom on Twitter at @thomasstiehm.

Summary provided by Sylvia Fronczak.

Go to bit.ly/2020addo-stiehm to watch the entire presentation.

DevSecOps Journey in DoD Enterprise

*presented by Hasan Yasar and
Nicolas Chaillan*

CHAPTER 48

DevSecOps Journey in DoD Enterprise

The Department of Defense (DoD) depends on software, but it doesn't always control development. Instead, they must maintain software written elsewhere. Difficulties arise when the entire lifecycle is out of their hands.

Why is that? Well, when comparing DoD against the private sector, the DoD starts with acquisition. They purchase software that must later be integrated with all their existing systems. Surprisingly, they have more resources than the private sector, but they end up with less productivity. Because of these limitations, there's also less agility.

Another result of using software developed elsewhere, they must worry about latent cyber vulnerabilities. These vulnerabilities put the DoD at risk.

Because of this ecosystem, they must work differently.

Issues the DoD Faces

So what sort of problems does DoD experience from that acquisition-based ecosystem?

First, development is a heavy waterfall process in every phase of the software development lifecycle. So when looking at the system with a DevOps perspective, things become difficult. All the timelines are extended. In fact, sometimes it takes years to identify errors in the system.

Additionally, they experience integration difficulties. The testing is all manual, and configuration changes are extensive. To add more pain, they lack parity between their dev, integration, and prod environments.

Changing the Culture and Systems

There are may barriers to culture change. For one, the DoD cannot fail fast, nor can they fail in production, as the results could be devastating.

Additionally they must integrate and manage hundreds of applications. More on the culture side, they lack the iterative and incremental mindset that many companies have developed.

Their organizational structure creates additional barriers through excessive silos of knowledge. Systems are based on organizational structure.

And then pushing to production creates additional issues. They're unable to push to production as often as private organizations.

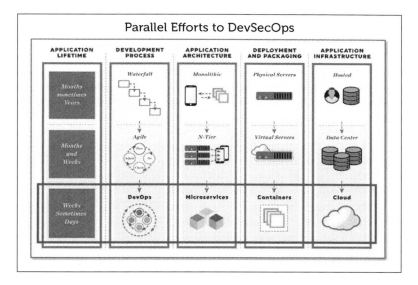

How the DoD Is Implementing DevSecOps

So what's the DoD enterprise DevSecOps initiative? First, the DevSecOps stack is open source and open to the public. Everything is Infrastructure -as-Code. And the stack can run on any environment, by leveraging Kubernetes. They also harden the K8S environment as much as possible.

The DoD brings enterprise IT capabilities with Cloud One and Platform One into the organization as well. This provides better onboarding and support for the teams.

Furthermore, they've standardized metrics and defined acceptable thresholds for all of the DoD.

They're also providing training with self-learning capabilities with state of the art DevSecOps curriculum. In fact, they train over 100,000 people a year.

To make all this happen, they have built DevSecOps layers that all include continuous monitoring and infrastructure as code. The layers span from the application layers of the development teams all the way to the infrastructure layer.

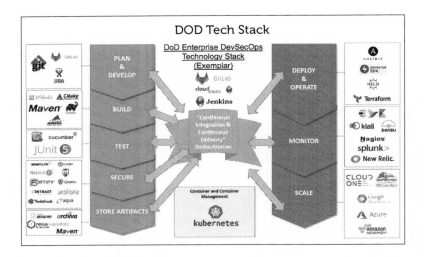

In the DoD tech stack, they include continuous integration and continuous delivery as the core. Then, around that, they build upon stacks of tools for both building and operating their applications.

For security, the DoD uses a sidecar container security stack. This includes continuous scanning, alerting, and behavior detection with Twistlock. For container security and insider threat, they use Anchor for detecting changes in their Docker files.

In conclusion, the DoD feels that if Kubernetes is good enough for their weapons systems, it's definitely good enough for your business. ∎

ABOUT THE PRESENTERS

Hasan Yasar is the Interim Director of Lifecycle Innovation & Automation group in the SSD Division of the Software Engineering Institute, CMU. Hasan leads an engineering group on software development processes and methodologies, specifically on DevOps and development and cloud technologies, and big data problems while providing expertise and guidance to SEI's clients. Hasan has more than 25 years experience as senior security engineer, software engineer, software architect and manager in all phases of secure software development and information modeling processes. He specializes in secure software solutions design and development experience in the cybersecurity domain including data-driven investigation and collaborative incident management, network security assessment, automated, large-scale malware triage/ analysis, medical records management, accounting, simulation systems and document management. He is also an adjunct faculty member in CMU Heinz College and Institute of Software Research where he currently teaches "Software and Security" and "DevOps: Engineering for Deployment and Operations."

Mr. Nicolas Chaillan, a highly qualified expert, is appointed as the first U.S. Air Force Chief Software Officer, under Dr. William Roper, the Assistant Secretary of the Air Force for Acquisition, Technology and Logistics, Arlington, Virginia. He is also the co-lead for the Department of Defense Enterprise DevSecOps Initiative with the Department of Defense Chief Information Officer. As the Air Force's senior software czar, Mr. Chaillan is responsible for enabling Air Force programs in the transition to Agile and DevSecOps to establish force-wide DevSecOps capabilities and best practices, including continuous Authority to Operate processes and faster streamlined technology adoption.

Mr. Chaillan is recognized as one of France's youngest entrepreneurs after founding WORLDAKT at 15 years of age. He has founded 12 companies including AFTER-MOUSE.com, Cyber Revolution, Prevent Breach, and anyGuest.com, among others. Over the last eight years alone, he created and sold over 180 innovative software products to 45 Fortune 500 companies. Additionally, he is recognized as a pioneer of the computer language PHP. You can find Nicolas on Twitter at @NicolasChaillan.

Summary provided by Sylvia Fronczak.

Go to bit.ly/2020addo-yasar to watch the entire presentation.

Voices of All Day DevOps, Volume 2

FEEDBACK LOOPS

Like what you've read?

View the sessions at
www.alldaydevops.com/ondemand

ALL DAY DEVOPS